D0844035

AN IMMIGRANT'S DAUGHTER

*A Biography
of
Molly Miyako Kimura*

BY KAREN WILSON

ACKNOWLEDGEMENTS

The author and Molly Kimura wish to thank Hiroko Tsuda, Rhonda Butcher and Stuart Ito for giving generously of their time and talent to make this project possible. Left to right: Karen Wilson, Hiroko Tsuda, Molly Miyako Kimura, Stuart Ito.

Cover image by Kashu Yoshikawa.

PROLOGUE

History is best told through stories. Every family has one. For immigrant families, the story is of two cultures, two languages, and the telling is complex. For Japanese immigrant families incarcerated during World War II simply because of who they were, words like courage, perseverance and faith seem inadequate to describe what has been required of them.

What were the challenges and the opportunities ahead for the Nisei, the second generation of Japanese immigrants? American citizens, they had a chance to mold a new life after the War Relocation Authority camps. They had no choice but to do so. They began with what they had. For Molly Miyako Kimura, that was a deep Buddhist faith, an all-encompassing love of her culture, and a family with high expectations and an entrepreneurial streak. She has woven those attributes into a life full of unexpected turns and joys.

When I first met Molly Kimura she was approaching 70. Like most people, I was immediately struck by her enthusiasm for life. Her mind and her movements were quick. She did not waste time or words. As her Ikebana student I had to work to grasp the finer points behind an apparently simple arrangement. Molly was exacting.

Throughout her life she has been able to focus on a goal until she achieves it, regardless of the time or effort involved. Telling her story is the work of this part of Molly's life. And so we sat down, many times, to pull out the stories she wanted to tell.

Where I could, I researched the stories Molly told. In every case I found her memory was superb. Molly's head is full of stories, and as she tells them she leaps through time and across continents. She is in a hurry to tell how the stories end. It is, in all ways, hard to keep up, but the rewards of listening to Molly are profound.

Karen Wilson

FOREWORD

It has been seventy-two years since Molly and I met in the Tule Lake Relocation Center in 1942. It was during the World War II evacuation of people of Japanese ancestry following President Franklin D. Roosevelt's Executive Order 9066. Both of our families were relocated from Northern California to Block 43 in Ward V. I was eight years old and she was eighteen. Because all the people of the same block shared community mess halls, laundry, shower, bathing and toilet facilities, Molly and I would encounter each other often and we became acquainted. Even at that age, I observed that Molly had a special eloquence about her, which engendered awe and respect.

Molly Miyako Kimura was a very obedient daughter of Mr. and Mrs. Nobujiro Nakamura, immigrants from the Hiroshima Prefecture. She became the ideal culmination of the upbringing by an intensely strict yet compassionate, religious mother, a highly successful business-owner father, and her character-molding, progressive elder sister, Helen. Molly was the fourth child in a family of five children, four girls and a boy. Helen and her mother mentored her by giving her direction and encouraging her to take specific roads to enhance her education and training.

While being held in the War Relocation Authority camp, Molly's parents led their family by setting an example, maintaining their optimistic hope for a better tomorrow without bitterness toward the U.S. Government. Concerned with the spiritual education of the children in the camps, Molly and her friends opened the Ward V Buddhist Sunday School (now called Dharma School). I enrolled in the fourth grade Dharma (Teachings of the Buddha) class. Molly was my first Dharma school teacher. She and her co-teachers taught by using mimeographed picture stories to illustrate the Buddha's teachings. Thus, my quest for spiritual attainment had begun, and Molly became my mentor.

By studying Japanese language and cultural arts intensely, Molly evolved into a unique, highly honored bilingual, bicultural unofficial ambassador, bridging the divergent cultures of the people of Japan and the United States. She trained diligently as a musician in the ancient Japanese lute, the Biwa; achieved the highest master's level in Ikenobo, the art of flower arranging, and became a certified teacher in the Yoshikawa art of sand painting. At age sixty-nine she began a three-year Japanese correspondence course to study Jodo Shinshu (the Nembutsu teachings — essence of enlightenment) religion, and upon graduation, at age 75, was ordained as a Jodo Shinshu Minister by Monshu Koshin Ohtani at the Nishi Hongwanji in Kyoto. At the delicate age of 90, she eagerly conducts memorial services monthly at the Sacramento Buddhist Church, encourages Dharma talks in her home, and enjoys giving flower-arranging classes in her home.

She has received many accolades, awards and certificates of accomplishment, and has been interviewed by journalists. She considers her most noteworthy accomplishments to be the State of California Standard Designated Teaching Credential of Adult Education, Valid for Life from August 1975 in the Subject or Field of Japanese Culture and or Customs, Flower Arranging and Related Technology; having taught for thirty years in the Sacramento Dharma School and having served as both Superintendent of the school and as a Superintendent of the Northern California Dharma School Teachers League. For all her community service, Molly Miyako Kimura has been recognized in a special section in the Sacramento History Section of the Central Library of the Sacramento Public Library.

Molly has created a legacy for future generations of Japanese Americans to emulate. She has demonstrated that studying and learning the Japanese language and traditional cultural arts will only enhance not lessen a person's character building. This will help to strengthen peaceful interpersonal and international relationships both here and abroad.

It has been my great privilege and an honor to call Molly Miyako Kimura my mentor and close friend.

Hiroko Tsuda
Past President,
Buddhist Churches of America Federation Buddhist Women's Associations

CHAPTER ONE

From Hiroshima to Northern California

Molly Miyako Kimura is proud to say she is an immigrant's daughter. Her American success story begins in a time of global cultural and economic change that sent her parents' generation on a long and difficult journey. Nobujiro Nakamura and Motoyo Takayama were born in the late 1800s, just as profound shifts in Japan's economy and political structure were beginning to sweep aside two centuries of rigid Tokugawa Shogunate rule. Their ancestral homes were in Hiroshima Prefecture. At the time of their birth, it was peaceful farmland. By the time they approached young adulthood at the beginning of the twentieth century, Nobujiro and Motoyo, and thousands of their generation, were forced to look far from home for opportunity; they joined a wave of Japanese immigrants to all parts of the world.

Commodore Matthew C. Perry, representing the U.S. government, signed the Convention of Kanagawa on March 31, 1854. The treaty forced Japan's doors open to the worldwide network of labor, capital and transportation. Molly's grandmother, whose husband was a wig maker for the Samurai, told her grandchildren half a century later how she longed to make the trip from Hiroshima to Yokohama to see Perry's four "black ships," the name the Japanese applied to all Western ships for the smoke bellowing from their coal-powered engines. The four hundred-mile journey to the western side of the island of Honshu was too long for her to make, but the black ships continued to stir her imagination for many years.

The transition from an insular island nation to a global power was a tumultuous time for both Japan and its people. Even before Perry's arrival, members of the elite Samurai class had been undergoing changes; they were becoming civil servants and merchants. The rigid class distinctions that held the Shogunate together were deteriorating. Some of the Samurai saw opportunity in the economic and political upheaval forced on Japan by its introduction to the West. Citing outrage over the Shogunate's capitulation to foreigners, a group of noblemen and young Samurai mounted a civil war (the Boshin War) to bring the imperial court back to political power. Fourteen year-old Prince Mutsuhito took the throne in 1867, beginning a new era, named Meiji, meaning "enlightened rule." Molly's parents were born during the Meiji Restoration, which lasted until 1912 and encompassed the first half of the Empire of Japan. The new Japanese government described its intentions in the slogan "rich country, strong army." Kure, Hiroshima's port, became an important military site. Farmers were taxed to pay for growth in the manufacturing and industrial sectors. The first stirrings of Japanese nationalism spread rapidly. As preparations ramped up for the 1894-95 War with China (known as the First Sino-Japanese War), it became clear that all available men would soon be drafted into the military.

Japanese immigration to the U.S. began in northern California with a small group of the Samurai class who had supported the Shogun in the Boshin War, and feared retribution from the Emperor. In 1869, twenty-two Samurai fled to the Gold Hill Ranch in El Dorado County, east of Sacramento. They brought with them mulberry trees, tea plant seeds, fruit tree saplings, rice, bamboo and other crops to establish the Wakamatsu Tea and Silk Farm Colony. It was a short-lived experiment. Drought, competition for water and withdrawal of financial support from one of its well-connected founders contributed to its demise in 1871. Today the area is a state historic site and the National Park Service has recognized it as nationally significant. Although the Wakamatsu experiment failed, it revealed

1908: Molly's father, Nobujiro Nakamura, in the barbershop in what is now Third Street in Old Sacramento.

the possibilities that northern California held for Japanese immigrants. The Wakamatsu land lies only fourteen miles from Marysville, where, a quarter century later, the Nakamura brothers were to settle and raise families.

Large scale Japanese labor migration began in 1868, when an American businessman, Eugene M. Van Reed, recruited and sent a group of about one hundred fifty Japanese to work in slave-like conditions on sugar plantations in Hawaii. This unauthorized recruitment and shipment of laborers is known as the *gannenmono*. Treatment of the migrants was so bad that the Meiji government banned such immigration for more than twenty-five years. The government was forced to reconsider as poverty in Japan became more widespread and severe, and the population grew beyond the limits of what the island nation could support. The Immigration Convention of 1885 led to an agreement between the government of Japan and the Kingdom of Hawaii, as well as subsequent agreements between the leaders of neighboring Hiroshima and Yamaguchi Prefectures and the

1909: Molly's father Nobujiro. This is the photo he exchanged with Motoyo.

owners of sugar plantations in Hawaii. About twenty-nine thousand Japanese traveled to Hawaii over the next nine years to work on sugar plantations under three-year contracts. Thousands also departed for Thursday Island, New Caledonia, Australia, Fiji, and other South Pacific destinations for similar contract work. These were not settlers, but *dekasegi*, laborers planning to return home with money after a few years of work in a foreign land.

This seemed like a good opportunity for thousands of Japanese men. While many planned to return, some laborers planned to work the sugar fields for as little as a year with a goal of entering the United States from Honolulu after their contracted time was up.

In 1904, Nobujiro Nakamura left his home and family in Asa Minamiku, Higashino, near Hiroshima City, and boarded a steamship for the sugar cane fields of Hawaii. He must have known at least some of the hardships that awaited him. From 1894 to 1908, approximately 125,000 Japanese migrants sailed to Hawaii. His older brother Buntaro had made the same trip a few years before.

Buntaro and Nobujiro weighed the risks: the month-long journey, and reports of terrible conditions on the sugar plantations; the poverty facing their families in Hiroshima, and the likelihood that they would be drafted into the military, leaving their families with no support. The Japanese government was encouraging both men and women to earn money abroad and then return to help their families. Many men from Hiroshima made the hard choice to risk the perils of a long sea voyage and anti-Asian sentiment in their ultimate destination, the United States.

It was a tradition in Japanese families for the oldest son to inherit the family land. Since Buntaro, the oldest son, and Nobujiro chose to emigrate, a third brother, Saiichi, stayed behind in Hiroshima to care for their grandmother, who was descended from the Fukushima clan. Saiichi had six sons. Two of them, including his oldest son, died on a Japanese Navy submarine during World War II. Another son was to receive help from his American cousins in attending the military academy at Kure.

In the sugar cane fields of Hawaii, the Nakamura brothers labored beside immigrants from China, the Philippines, Korea, Puerto Rico and Portugal. Japanese accounted for almost seventy percent of plantation workers in 1893, when a group of plantation owners overthrew the Hawaiian Monarchy. While the new Hawaiian government was looking for settlers, the planters wanted cheap workers. Hawaiian business agents approached the Japanese government with promises of free passage and decent wages and working conditions. Private companies were accused of taking advantage of immigrants by charging them high commissions for the trip. Loans to finance the voyage from Japan to Honolulu accrued twelve and a half percent interest. Before the ink had dried on the agreements, Hawaii's planters changed the terms, passing procurement and transportation costs on to the migrants and instituting harsh labor controls to maximize their returns.

In the fields, Nobujiro and his fellow workers endured injuries from razor-sharp cane leaves, the hot tropical sun and strict plantation rules requiring them to labor from sunup to sunset. From their wages of about fourteen dollars a month, seven or eight dollars were deducted to pay for sleeping quarters. These were sheds with as many as fifty people living together. Supervisors on horseback watched the workers constantly, and whipped anyone they thought might be shirking. A government report noted twenty strikes by Japanese plantation laborers during 1900 alone, involving a total of more than seven thousand eight hundred field hands, cane cutters and strippers, and mill workers. Nobujiro never talked about these days afterward, but it is likely that he and Buntaro knew about the strikes, even though they were not actually participants. A young man in the prime of his physical strength, Nobujiro was able to endure these hardships as a necessary step toward a better future. His purpose in life was to make as much money as possible no matter what it took, and then to return to Hiroshima and set up a household of his own. But it was here that he made himself a promise never again to work as a field laborer.

In 1905, Nobujiro again followed Buntaro, this time to the hop fields of the northern Sacramento Valley near Wheatland. Buntaro had immigrated in 1900 to one of the first farms in northern California to hire Japanese immigrants, the Emil Clemons Horst Ranch. Steamship companies were recruiting immigrants to work for hops ranches, and this may have been how the Nakamura brothers financed their voyages. They likely lived in tents erected for seasonal workers in Horstville, a company town near Wheatland. Chinese immigrants formed the first work force on the hops ranches. Tens of thousands of Chinese had arrived in California during the Gold Rush and stayed to work on the Central Pacific, and then on the Transcontinental Railroads. Most were left unemployed when the railroad work ran out, but the railroad opened new markets for crops that grew in fertile northern California soil, and Chinese laborers were quickly recruited to work in the new agricultural fields.

Economic conditions in the U.S. were depressed following the Civil War; there was stiff competition for even the lowest-paying jobs. Chinese workers were sometimes called in to break strikes, and anti-Asian sentiment, always present, often led to violence against Chinese workers in Northern California. Many cases involving agricultural workers were never documented. But some were, and they paint the picture. In 1886, a group of thirty masked men from Wheatland rounded up Chinese American workers on H. Roddan's ranch, beat eleven hop pickers, then burned down the Chinese workers' bunkhouse on C. D. Wood's ranch.

Responding to public outcry, Congress passed the Chinese Exclusion Act in 1882, prohibiting Chinese laborers from entering the U.S. It was not repealed until 1942. In 1907, Congress approved legislation allowing President Roosevelt to issue an executive order stopping the immigration of Japanese laborers from Hawaii and Mexico. Exclusion laws, and the anti-Chinese violence that followed, resulted in demand for another source of immigrant labor.

It was against this background that Japanese immigrants began arriving in California in the late 1880s. Census records show that in 1900 there were fewer than a thousand Japanese people over the age of fifteen in the U.S. By the time Nobujiro arrived in Northern California, the tiny community of Japanese immigrants was growing, and establishing a foothold. Living conditions for the field hands have been described as "abysmally unlivable." Growers took advantage wherever they could. Workers generally made less than a dollar fifty to three dollars a day for twelve hours of work under Sacramento Valley heat that could reach a hundred ten degrees. They lived in tents on a barren hillside and had to pay for the water they drank from irrigation canals contaminated with dysentery. In 1899 workers on the Horst Ranch, including a number of Japanese, quit and went on strike for higher pay. On the neighboring Durst Ranch, conditions reached the boiling point with the Wheatland Hop Riot of 1913, one of the first labor disturbances in California history. The California State militia was called in to break up the riot after the sheriff, the district attorney, and two workers were killed. In solidarity with their fellow workers, Japanese workers walked out at the beginning of the strike and withdrew from the area, in fear that their presence might cause the non-Japanese strikers to lose support. In 1915, Japanese farmers came together to create the Japanese Farmers Association. It offered Japanese farmers technical advice, assisted them in marketing their produce and promoted their agricultural interests. More than a thousand Northern California Japanese farmers were members in 1918.The Nakamura brothers established some of the first businesses serving these hard-working farmers and their families.

Demonstrating what became a lifelong ability to make the most of whatever opportunity presented itself, Nobujiro noted that Japanese bamboo rakes were not available anywhere around Wheatland. He wrote to Japan, ordered a supply and sold them to the Japanese workers. He also ordered Japanese medicines and sold them in the labor camps. Herbal medicine fulfilled an important health need in the nineteenth century. Western medicine had not yet developed anesthetics, vaccinations, or sophisticated surgical techniques. Patent medicines were widely used, and their contents were not regulated. Japanese herbal remedies had one to two thousand years of experience behind them, and were prized for their ability to cure or reduce the effects of a wide variety of ailments.

Nobujiro continued to offer traditional medicinal treatments for pneumonia at least into the 1920s. Molly recalls one incident: "When we were living in Yuba City, my father was asked to help a sick man. He visited the man at home, and brought a black carp for its blood. Just one or two tablespoons were needed. The sick man was okay after taking this blood. But he was ill a second time and they couldn't find the right fish."

Buntaro moved to Marysville, where by 1907 he owned a store and boarding house, and was making deliveries to Wheatland by horse and buggy. He and his wife Ichi offered their home for services conducted by a visiting Buddhist minister from Sacramento. Nobujiro's fledgling business ventures had allowed him to save a little money. He moved to Sacramento and served as an apprentice barber in the booming waterfront today called Old Sacramento. Barbering was the trade that allowed him to make enough money to think differently about his future. He decided to send for a wife.

In 1907, President Theodore Roosevelt and the government of Japan signed the Gentlemen's Agreement: the U.S. would stop issuing passports to Japanese citizens, but passports would continue to be issued for Japanese who had been in the U.S. previously and also to wives, parents and relatives of those already in the U.S.

1909: Molly's mother, Motoyo. This is the picture bride photo she exchanged with Nobujiro.

Knowing that all Japanese immigration was soon to stop (it did stop in 1924), Japanese bachelors set about to find suitable wives and bring them to the U.S. The result was an influx of more than twenty thousand Japanese "picture brides" by 1908.

Picture bride marriages were arranged through an intermediary. Where family ties were still strong, parents in Japan would invite a potential bride to come and live with them, as a test. Was she a hard worker? Was she was able to persevere? Was she smart enough to learn a foreign language? Was she patient? Nobujiro's mother was very strict. Motoyo Takayama was the third potential bride she tested for fitness as a *yome-san*, or daughter-in-law. The youngest of five sisters, Motoyo welcomed the chance to prove herself fit for a new life in the U.S. She passed the test. After photographs were exchanged, her marriage to Nobujiro was entered at the town registry in the city of Hiroshima. When she boarded a ship bound for the U.S., Motoyo was by Japanese custom already married to Nobujiro Nakamura although she had yet to meet him.

The Kaga Maru set sail from the Port of Kobe on March 12, 1909 and arrived at the Port of Seattle on April 5. The ship's manifest lists Motoyo Nakamura as a married woman. Her age was listed as twenty-one (she was actually nineteen), her "Calling or Occupation" as "Barber/None," her last permanent residence as Mikawa Mura, Hiroshima. The Kaga Maru's manifest included eleven other Japanese passengers. All attested they could meet the U.S. government's requirements: they could read and write English, each had fifty dollars in cash, and all the women were married.

1934: Molly's grandmother, Fukushima, in her vegetable garden in Hiroshima.

7

> ### Other passengers listed on the Kaga Maru's manifest for the voyage from the Port of Kobe to the Port of Seattle, March 12 – April 5, 1909:
>
> Kanejo Yoshida, female, age 28, farm laborer, from Hiroshima bound for Los Angeles
>
> Sono Fukuhara, female, age 21, laundress, from Wakayama bound for Salt Lake
>
> Yasumatsu Uruyama, male, age 15, cook from Hidaka bound for Seattle
>
> Ryuichi Yamamoto, male, age 17, laborer from Hiroshima bound for Los Angeles
>
> Hira Yoshihara, female, age 31, cook, from Hiroshima bound for Olympia
>
> Denjiro Yoshino, male, age 32, farm laborer from Hiroshima bound for Tacoma
>
> Mankichi Kamei, male, age 39, fisherman, from Kyoto bound for Frisco
>
> Yasu Hayashi, female, age 22, farm laborer, from Okayama bound for Spokane
>
> Shinta Kadona, male, age 17, farm laborer, from Yamaguchi bound for Richmond
>
> Shiye Matsushima, female, age 21, washerwoman, from Kumamoto bound for Seattle
>
> Masu Miyagawa, female, age 20, farm laborer, from Yamaguchi bound for Sacramento

Motoyo was more fortunate than many picture brides. Her husband was young and good-looking, wearing a Western style suit of clothes and a hat for their first meeting. Molly has often imagined that day. "At the Port of Seattle, my mother must have been holding the picture of my father, looking around. My father too, holding the picture trying to recognize each other. You know what my father told me? They all arrived in kimono! The women were all farmers' daughters. My father borrowed this big American suit with a hat. I guess he didn't know what to buy. They didn't have any women around." Many brides were not able to recognize their new husbands by the old photographs that had been sent to them. They found men much older, and much poorer, than they had been led to believe. But what could they do? They couldn't return to Japan. Stories tell of women who had the courage to walk out and find another man. Occasionally the surprise went the other way. Molly tells the story of a friend, a man about three years older than she is. "He's from Kyushu. When his picture bride came she was pregnant. What could he do? Funny thing, this one son didn't look like the rest of the siblings! It was an arranged marriage and you were stuck with the person usually. But if the woman was a go-getter she could find someone else."

Motoyo and Nobujiro held a wedding ceremony in a Seattle Buddhist church in September 1909. Although they were to be married for more than sixty years, Molly never learned much about her parents' wedding. The Nakamuras traveled by train from Seattle to Sacramento and began their married life with Nobujiro teaching his new wife the barbering trade. In this respect also Motoyo was fortunate. While she worked very hard in those first years, she escaped the harsh life that awaited many picture brides. Motoyo brought with her a strong, lifelong devotion to Buddhism. At home in Hiroshima, the Meiji era had brought a decades-long push to support Shrine Shinto as the country's dominant religion. Scholars note that part of this effort was a desire to make the people willing to accept higher taxes, and, ultimately, worship of the Emperor as a divine being. In this regard, Shrine Shinto reached the height of its success in the 1930s. Buddhists resisted the imposition of taxes to support Shinto shrines. They believed that religion was meant to be a spiritual quest focusing on morals and ethics, and not external manifestation of power. For Hiroshima's many devout Buddhist families, including Motoyo's family, the Takayamas, the discord created by the government's support for Shrine Shinto was added to the economic burdens of the

June, 1959: 50th Wedding Anniversary of Molly's parents, Mr. and Mrs. Nobujiro Nakamura. Seated (left to right): Motoyo Nakamura, Sylvia Kimura, Nobujiro Nakamura. 2nd Row: Nancy Maruyama (Katherine's daughter); Molly's sister Katherine; Toshi Kawamura (Katherine's daughter) with baby Julie Kawamura; Molly; Marie Tsukimoto (daughter of a close family friend in Japan, married from the Nakamura's home); Molly's sister Helen Iwasaki; Albert Tsukimoto in front of Helen; Marjorie Iwasaki-Nakaji. 3rd Row: Katherine's husband Tom Sato; Goro Kawamura with baby Matthew; Kaz with baby Clifford; Joe Nakamura; George Iwasaki.

times. Her strong faith became a lifeline for Motoyo and her daughters as they faced even more difficult times in their new country.

Molly is proud of her parents, and their accomplishments in the face of hardships that would continue for most of their lives. She credits them with instilling in her the faith that helped her move ahead in the face of difficulties. "Growing up, I heard people say, 'You are immigrants' children,' like an insult," Molly says. "It was the economy in Hiroshima that forced people to emigrate. They were sharecroppers. The farmers gave a share of their crops to the lords. Why mention it? Many people in the U.S. have a common story. We are all immigrants' children."

1980: The Kimura family: Clifford, Kaz, Molly and Sylvia

1971: Sylvia and Kaz at her graduation from U.C. Berkeley.

CHAPTER TWO

An Abiding Child

In the year Miyako Nakamura was born, the memory of the Gold Rush was still alive in Marysville. Founded in 1850, the town was named for Mary Covillaud, a survivor of the infamous Donner party. She had been rescued just three years before from one of the most spectacular tragedies in the history of Western migration. Her husband, Charles Covillaud, discovered gold in the nearby fields and helped to lay out the new town. Located forty miles north of Sacramento on the bank of the Feather River, Marysville was a stopping point for riverboats from Sacramento and San Francisco carrying miners on their way to the digging grounds. By 1857 its strategic location had made it one of the largest cities in California, with a population of almost ten thousand. More than ten million dollars in gold was shipped from Marysville to the U.S. Mint in San Francisco. The town boasted of mills, iron works, factories, machine shops, schools, churches and two daily newspapers. Its citizens dreamed that Marysville would become "The New York of the Pacific." But the very advantages that had helped it grow forever limited its dreams. Debris from upriver hydraulic mining raised the riverbed by as much as ten feet. Riverboats could no longer make the trip up from San Francisco and Sacramento. Flooding was much more frequent and severe. The city built a levee system, still in place today, that sealed it off and made further growth almost impossible. Marysville became known as "California's Oldest 'Little' City," and up to World War II, "The Peach Bowl City."

Chinese immigrants once called Marysville the "Third City," after San Francisco and Sacramento in importance. Its thriving Chinese community included a temple located at the foot of the river levee, and several blocks of businesses and fraternal organizations. A relatively brief period of co-existence with the Caucasian community came to an end in 1886, when anti-Asian sentiment turned to violence. White residents forcibly uprooted and expelled the Chinese from Marysville. But the nearby hops fields depended on immigrant labor, which local residents were forced to recognize. Another period of relative calm in interracial relations allowed Japanese immigrants to set up shops and homes in an area adjacent to what remained of the Chinese community. Marysville's Japantown, or Nihon-machi, was also built up against the levee, within a few hundred feet of the fearsome Feather River.

The Nakamura family lived in Marysville during the years when its Japanese population peaked. Before World War II, about four hundred Japanese people, Issei (first generation) and Nisei (second generation), lived in Yuba County, and three hundred lived in Yuba City, in neighboring Sutter County. Yuba City never developed a Nihon-machi, so families living there crossed the river to Marysville for services and supplies. About twenty Japanese businesses served the two communities. In 2012, the Marysville Library asked Molly to help fill in the historical gaps in information about pre-World War II Japanese-owned businesses. She remembered them all. They included the Toyo Hotel at Second and C Streets, with accommodation for twenty boarders and guests. Nearby was the Kamiya Laundry. Molly's uncle Buntaro owned the B. Nakamura Company Boarding House and Grocery, as well as a barbershop and bathhouse in an adjoining building. The bathhouse consisted of four tubs in separate rooms with one huge water heater to serve all of them. Other businesses were the Yamamoto Pool Hall, located near the Hiraoka General Store, Hashimoto Dry Goods Store and Ice Cream Shop, Taketa Shoe Repair and the Furuta and Maruyama confectioneries. The Toyoda Barbershop served Caucasian, Hispanic and African American customers in addition to Japanese. Like most Japantown barbering establishments, it included *o-furo* (baths) and a shower. The two-story Okimoto Building, still standing behind the Silver Dollar Saloon, served as a boarding house for transient workers. Japanese immigrants were forbidden by law to own property, so business owners began by renting. Only a lucky few were eventually able to buy the land under their stores.

Nobujiro and Motoyo began their family while they were still working as apprentice barbers in Old Sacramento. Their first child, Helen, was born in Sacramento in 1910. She was the first American citizen in the family. Nobujiro was beginning to feel the symptoms of a heart ailment that was to become serious. He moved his young family to live near Buntaro, who was at this time a foreman on the Wheatland Hops Ranch near Marysville. A second daughter, Sumiyo, born in Marysville two years later, succumbed to the flu as an infant. Katherine, the family's third daughter, was born in 1915. Soon afterward, Nobujiro's heart ailment became life threatening. "My father had a strong spirit, but a weak constitution," Molly says. "To recover his health, he took the family back to his parents' home in Hiroshima Prefecture, to the house where he was born. They lived with my grandmother and uncle for three to five years while my father recuperated. My grandmother always noticed that my sisters called my father 'papa' and my mother 'mama.' In Japan you're supposed to say 'otosan' and 'okaasan,' meaning father and mother. He saw doctors there, and got well. My sister said grandma was very strict. Even though they had white rice, my grandmother would serve the family genmai, rice mixed with wheat, for health." When her parents returned to the U.S., they followed a custom of the time by leaving Helen, their first born, behind to receive her education in Japanese schools. Helen lived with her grandmother until she graduated from high school, when she returned to the U.S.

In 1920, shortly after their return, the family farmed land near Yuba City. Miyako was born at home on March 1, 1924. Joseph, the only son in the family, was born on January 21, 1927. The small farm was located between the two bridges built to join Marysville and Yuba City, and beside the 1870s era levee. "My father didn't like farming, so my mother did that work, raising mostly vegetables, while my father sold the produce," Molly says. Her neighbors included the Murata family from Kumamoto Prefecture. One of their six children became a nationally prominent geologist. Kiguma Jack Murata, born in 1909, was a volcanologist who made significant contributions to the science of the 1959-60 eruption of Kilauea Volcano in Hawaii, as well as marine fossil formations in California and Oregon.

The California Alien Land Law was enacted in 1913, forbidding "aliens ineligible for citizenship" from purchasing, and later from leasing property. Since Asians were the only immigrants ineligible for naturalization under U.S. immigration laws, the phrase "aliens ineligible for citizenship" became a legal way for states to limit the rights of Asian immigrants without targeting a group racially in the language of the law. Many states passed such laws, including Arizona, Arkansas, Florida, Idaho, Louisiana, Minnesota, Montana, Nebraska, New Mexico, Oregon, Texas, Utah, Washington, and Wyoming. The U.S. Supreme Court ruled alien land laws unconstitutional in 1952. The California Alien Land Law was strengthened in 1920 to prohibit the transfer of land to noncitizens by sale or lease. Aliens ineligible for citizenship could not hold land in guardianship for their children who were citizens. If it was determined that land was purchased in one person's name, but with money from an Asian alien, the land would automatically become state property. Fortunately for many Japanese families, including Molly's, evasions of the 1920 law were largely ignored. Nobujiro waited for Helen to return from Japan, and purchased property in her name to secure his businesses. The Nakamuras moved to Marysville shortly after Joe was born. They lived in a small rental house on B Street. Nobujiro built a small store where he sold gasoline and Singer treadle sewing machines. As soon as he was able, he bought the house and donated part of the land for a Buddhist church.

Molly grew up regarding Helen, fourteen years her senior, as an authority figure and a source of advice and comfort. A toddler when Helen returned home, Molly absorbed the family pride in Helen's status as a top student in the family's homeland: "In those days the most brilliant student was captain of the class. In America I guess the most popular student would be elected, like a class president, but in Japan it was the most brilliant. My sister was captain through high school." Molly didn't speak English until she started kindergarten. When her teacher, Miss Reisinger, couldn't pronounce "Miyako" it was Helen who said, "Just call her Molly."

Helen became a participant in the family businesses. She helped as a bookkeeper while living in the Marysville house, and attended adult education classes to learn English. For many years she served as a Marysville reporter for the *Nichi Bei Times*, a newspaper published in San Francisco. (Disbanded after sixty-three years in 2009, the *Nichi Bei* Times was reorganized as the Nichi Bei Foundation and *Nichi Bei* Weekly.) In 1934, Helen returned to Japan for the Pan-Pacific Young Buddhist Association Conference. Most members of the Northern California group had just graduated from high school. Helen served as the Women's Director. On this trip Helen purchased the bell that still hangs in the courtyard of the Marysville Buddhist Church. The two-month trip included twenty days aboard ship, and took her to Manchuria, where she observed Japanese military training. This show of Japanese national strength impressed her enough to take several photographs. Just three years earlier, in 1931, a contingent of rogue Japanese military leaders staged a bombing of the South Manchuria Railway and blamed the incident on China. Japan seized control of Manchuria and installed a pro-Japanese government. Known as the Manchurian Incident, it was a pretext for the Japanese invasion of northern China. (Manchuria was restored to China after World War II, following a brief takeover by Russia.) Traveling in Asia in 1934, Helen was witnessing global events that would have an immense impact on her family within the next decade.

Like her father, Helen took advantage of opportunities that came her way. She was the first Japanese American woman to complete beauty school in Marysville. Nobujiro added a room onto the house, and Helen operated a beauty parlor as her own business. George Iwasaki, a young man with similar ideas about getting ahead in America, caught her eye. The two met through Young Buddhist Association events. The Iwasaki family leased farmland in West Sacramento. As the result of a childhood accident on the farm, George was not physically able to join the family business. His parents sent him to Japan to attend high school in Kyoto. When he returned to the U.S., they sent him to pharmacy school at the University of San Francisco. While George and his sister attended college, his four brothers became farmers in Clarksburg.

George's education was the best of what both Japan and the U.S. had to offer, and made him an attractive prospect. "My sister had high ideals," Molly says, "to marry only a professional. There were not many Nisei professionals."

Following Japanese custom, George's parents checked with cousins in Japan to see how the Nakamura family was doing before consenting to the marriage. "My family was more lenient; they didn't do that," Molly says. Helen and George were married in 1938.

Like his peers, George struggled to find work in the brief years between his graduation and the World War II incarceration of West Coast Japanese. The couple had a daughter, Marjorie. After the war, Helen and George moved to Columbus, Ohio for a few years so that George could find work. Throughout her life, wherever she was, Helen's presence in the Nakamura family was always strongly felt.

During her youngest years, when Molly's father operated a barbershop and bathhouse in Marysville, the whole family often pitched in to help with the business. For the first three years of her life, Molly's parents, busy with their own business and community life, found her a babysitter. The sitter was one of the first to remark that Molly demonstrated a good singing voice as she learned Japanese folk songs.

Molly recalls this incident from her childhood: "In those days there were Japanese casinos, all called Tokyo Club, in Sacramento, Marysville, San Francisco and Los Angeles, everywhere. There was a casino across from my father's store on C Street. In those days they had a secret gambling joint run by a hard gang. There was a man called Mr. Kagawa who was the leader of the casino in Marysville. He loved children, but he didn't have any. My father had a barbershop in the alley between B and C Streets. It had a public bath in the back. I remember playing in the barbershop. I was six. I was very quiet but I was very stubborn. This man used to come through the alley every day, and would stop in to tease me. I still remember playing in the waiting room when he came in. He would bend down and rub my scalp so hard that it hurt. One time when he did this I had had enough, and I was so mad that I hit him with a Coca Cola bottle. He got a big black eye. When he went back, his gang said, 'Hey, who did this?' He was so embarrassed, but he finally had to confess, 'Miyako struck me with a Coke bottle.' What could they do to a six year-old girl? Otherwise they would have extracted revenge. I was gutsy, don't you think? I remember him well. He was very quiet, with lots of dignity and a beautiful wife."

Nobujiro's business sense and ambition were outgrowing the barbershop. He became the first Japanese to sell Desoto and Plymouth cars in Northern California. Molly recalls those days: "My father had a vision of putting up a building and becoming a car dealer. But he couldn't because he was alien. This was very common. But Japanese customers did not feel comfortable doing business for such a large purchase with anyone except a Japanese businessman. My father traveled all over Northern California and sometimes as far as San Jose, taking orders from Japanese customers. The cars were delivered to the James Waters dealership on Van Ness Avenue in San Francisco. Once a month he would pick them up and drive them back for delivery. I can remember many drives with my father and brother crossing the Carquinez Bridge. The toll was twenty-five cents per person, which was a lot in those days, so my father had us duck down and hide on the floor of the back seat. 'Hide! Hide! Hide!' he would say as we approached the tollbooth. He sold cars only to Japanese. He told me when they first had the Model T Ford, there were no regular highways, so it took him four hours to drive the forty miles from Marysville to Sacramento."

Her father built a combination fifty-car showroom and garage at 1117 C Street in Marysville, with a house for the family behind it. He offered car repairs, gas and oil, and parking, since in those early days there were no driveways and no parking spaces on the street. Molly and Joe grew up playing in and around the big automobiles that came and went outside their front door. She remembers these as happy days for her family. She and her friends walked together down D Street to Marysville Elementary School. An organ played as the pupils marched up the steps to begin the school day. Walter Kernick was Principal. Lunch was ten cents in the cafeteria, which was in the basement of the three-story school. Molly looked forward to stopping at Woolworth's on the way home to buy candy. She and her friends passed Ellis Lake on the way, where laborers were working to turn a swampy Feather River spillway into a manmade lake designed by Robbie McLaren, designer of Golden Gate Park in San Francisco. Molly graduated from elementary school on June 10, 1938. The Japanese community in Marysville was

growing. Shibai, a theater group, presented traditional plays. Students celebrated Hanamatsuri, the flower festival, and Hinamatsuri, Girls' Day, and New Year's Day. The annual Obon Festival, which has been celebrated in Marysville for over a hundred years, featured female dancers celebrating and honoring those who came before, by telling traditional stories through dance and song accompanied by taiko drums.

1938: Molly, dressed in ceremonial robe at the celebration of the new Buddhist Church in Marysville.

1931: Molly, age 7, in Marysville during the 49er Celebration Parade, wearing a costume sewn by her older sister Helen.

Families attended Methodist and Buddhist churches. Molly was not yet five when her father and uncle donated the land and began to raise funds to build a Buddhist church. "My father always wanted to be in the background, he never wanted to be in the front," Molly says. "He hated to be a public speaker. He was always on the board but not president. My uncle was also a quiet man." For several years, a minister traveled from Sacramento to Marysville to conduct services. In 1938, the Marysville Buddhist Church became independent from the Sacramento Buddhist Church. Molly recalls that her father brought in a minister from Walnut Grove. She was twelve years old when the minister's wife, Mrs. Tarakawa, introduced her to Ikebana, the Japanese art of flower arranging. An ancient art thought to have reached Japan with Buddhist practices in the sixth century, Ikebana teaches awareness of humanity's relation to nature. Helen, who had studied Ikebana in high school in Japan, encouraged Molly to learn. It was the beginning of a lifelong devotion.

Molly began Japanese language lessons at the age of three, just a year after ground was broken on Marysville's first Gakuen (Japanese school) in 1926. For close to fifteen years, she went to Japanese language school every day. "On Saturday, language school was held for people who lived in the country," she recalls, "but in town we went every day after public school. Colusa had a Japanese language school, but Chico didn't have too many storeowners and farmers, so

1934: Molly, age ten, in her first Chikuzen Biwa recital, at Marysville Buddhist Church Hall. Her instructor was Kyokuso Yamamoto of San Francisco.

17

they used to come to Marysville. We had about two hundred students in the school. Japanese people had big families. Six to eight children were an average family. Some had as many as fifteen. Children from families that big seemed kind of rough to me. I guess they had to be to survive among fifteen children!"

Her teacher, Mrs. Chiharu Goda, an Issei, helped her learn English by translating Japanese language lessons into English. Molly recalls that Mrs. Goda was one of the few teachers of Japanese language in the U.S. at that time: "Our teacher couldn't speak English but she encouraged us to do so. In those days, with fear of war being declared, there was a need for bilingual speakers of Japanese and English."

Another of Molly's teachers was Kyokuso Yamamoto, who introduced her to another lifelong pursuit, the classical Japanese biwa. Biwa refers to both the instrument, a short-necked fretted lute, and to the classical songs it accompanies. In Buddhism, the biwa is the chosen instrument of Benten, goddess of music, eloquence, poetry, and education. Chikuzen biwa, the style Molly studied, was used by Buddhist monks visiting private residences to perform memorial services, as well as to relate entertaining stories and news. "When I was ten, I started learning biwa. It has been said that biwa is like opera. It combines music and history. You must be able to sing solo for long times at a stretch. One song can be twenty-five minutes long. We shortened it for demonstrations because it's too long for U.S. audiences. The stories are about famous educators, warriors, the Manchurian Incident, everything, all the history of Japan. Learning the biwa opened Japanese culture to me and stimulated my lifelong interest.

"There were ten girls in Mrs. Yamamoto's music class at that time. She lived in San Francisco and she came to Marysville on Sunday to teach. She was interested in the biwa, so she screened all her students to see if she thought we could learn, because it was so difficult. She said, 'Unless you can sing as well as learn the instrument, I would recommend you learn the piano instead.' She was a very dedicated artist in my instrument. She said I showed an aptitude for music, and that was when I started to go to San Francisco for private lessons. In those days my friend Setsuko Hayashi (now Ishikawa) and I could go all the way to the city together by ourselves, even though I was only about twelve. I still remember the fare for children was one dollar and ninety cents on the Sacramento Northern Railway from Marysville to San Francisco.

"The Bay Bridge was completed in 1936. Before that there was a ferry from Oakland to the Ferry Building in San Francisco. The Sacramento Northern Railway started in Chico, and the station was only two blocks away from my home in Marysville. From Marysville the train would come to Sacramento and pick up passengers, then go over the Carquinez Bridge. We could see people building the Bay Bridge. I still remember everything. While we waited for the ferryboat at Benecia we would go into the store and I would get an U-No bar, which I loved. We had to wear a hat and gloves, even in the summertime. Never white shoes going to San Francisco. San Francisco people never wore white shoes. I still remember the hats I had.

"During summer vacations we would stay at Mrs. Yamamoto's house at 1570 Post Street for up to a month. My friend Setsuko was two years older, and she loved to roam around Market Street. We would take a streetcar from Japantown, Post Street to Market Street. Buddy Uno was a U.C. Berkeley graduate who was the first Japanese to get a journalism degree. He took us to a fancy restaurant on Market Street, where they brought us finger bowls. Buddy told us, 'Don't drink it!' I was a country girl and nobody explained it to us! We said, 'Are we going to drink from this bowl? We have a cup for drinking!'"

March 31, 1940: Students of Kyokuso Yamamoto at a Chikuzen Biwa concert in Gyosei Hall, San Francisco. Molly and her fellow Marysville student Setsuko Hayashi performed; their parents, Mr. and Mrs. K. Hayashi, and Mrs. Motoyo Nakamura, attended.

On those trips to San Francisco, from 1934-1937, Molly absorbed some lessons from Buddy Uno that stayed with her for life. The famous Nisei journalist, whose column ran in *Rafu* and several other Bay Area papers, was born in Oakland and educated in Salt Lake City. He began his career in Los Angeles, and became active in the San Francisco Japanese American Citizens League in 1935. The Densho Encyclopedia notes that, "Like many older Nisei leaders, he embraced the bridge of understanding concept, 'that the Nisei had a special mission as American citizens to act as go-betweens between Japan and America.'" Though his own Japanese language skills were poor, he encouraged Nisei to go to Japan to improve their understanding of Japanese history and culture. Molly applied herself diligently to her biwa studies, earning the title Kyokuso while still a teenager. She remained lifelong friends with Setsuko, who went on to live in San Francisco after internment.

Molly's love of learning, established as a very young girl, has shaped her life. Many years later, she learned what happened to the first teacher who opened so many doors for her. "Mrs. Goda lived to be about ninety-five years old. She lived alone in Chicago. Her daughter died and her two grandchildren couldn't communicate in Japanese with their grandmother. Her husband died in the relocation camp. They were in Amache, Colorado, and he had health issues. If she had been bilingual she would have been able to communicate with her grandchildren. But she couldn't, and she died alone."

Molly was about twelve years old when her father's car dealership was "taken away due to prejudice" in 1937. "My father never stayed down for long. He was always looking for new things coming out. Gibson refrigerators were being introduced, and he had an opportunity to sell them. So he thought, 'Well, if they're going to take my dealership I might as well try something else.'" Nobujiro opened the Nakamura Company store in Sacramento. Still forbidden by law to own property, he continued to acquire it in Helen's name. The Nakamura Company was part of Sacramento's lively pre-World War II Japantown in the area between Third and Sixth Streets and M and Q Streets. In 1940, more than two hundred Japanese-owned businesses thrived in these few blocks.

Nobujiro sold appliances and other goods, including jewelry, and offered watch repair for Japanese customers. He was a creative marketer. His newspaper advertisements were in color in the early days of that technology, and he had a display of appliances at the 1940 State Fair. Young men and women eager to marry and start new households sought him out as a matchmaker. Many of his customers were strawberry and Tokay grape farmers from the Florin area. During these years he lived in a room in the back of his store on weekdays, and drove the forty miles home to his family in Marysville every weekend. When he could, he attended meetings of the County Planning Commission, keeping an eye on where development would be occurring in the next decade.

Japanese families gathered for social activities every month. Molly recalls: "They'd bring, in those days, ten dollars. Then after about eight months you'd be able to buy appliances. That was known as *tanomoshi*, mutual enjoyment. Then you'd bid for the pot and when you won, about once a year, you'd be able to buy something big. This went on until just a few years ago." Prefecture associations formed to celebrate the occasions marking community life, including holidays, birthdays and funerals. Extended families went on picnics and fishing trips together.

The Nakamuras often celebrated Molly's birthday with bento box picnics near Grass Valley in the hills of the Sierra Nevada. She recalls that at more than one picnic, an older, childless relative approached her parents about adopting Molly. This relative returned to Japan and opened a sewing school in Hiroshima, near the site where the atomic bomb was dropped in 1945.

During the Depression years, Molly recalls that some children from big farm families had no shoes. Her mother helped those who either appeared at the door or in other ways showed signs of needing food and clothing. "She was always compassionate. There was one lady who had a lot of children," Molly recalls. "She came with two live chickens asking my father to wait a while for payment of a debt." Her father was asked to take care of a friend's daughter, who was educated in Japan and came back to America. He found her jobs and kept an eye out for her safety. "A lot of Japanese wives didn't want to live in the U.S.," Molly says. "They took the children and went back to Japan while the father was left alone here to continue working and send money back to Japan. Many of these families appreciated my mother and father's kind help in this situation. On my mother's eighty-eighth birthday, one of the children my mother had helped during the Depression years came to her party with the traditional eighty-eight dollars made into a paper tree. For all that time, they remembered her help."

Nobujiro's diverse business dealings kept the family solvent during the Depression, maintaining close cultural ties to Japan while taking part in American life. Molly came to appreciate what turned out to be his wise business decisions during this time. "Once he had a family, my father wanted to stay in the U.S. Many Japanese, instead of investing in American land and property, bought Japanese stocks and invested in Japan through Sumitomo and Yokohama Banks. When war came, they lost everything."

Molly respected her father, though he was often away on business, and not always available nor especially warm toward his children. "I think of my dad as normal, but kind of strict," she recalls. "We were afraid to make him angry, my brother and myself. He always wore a custom made suit. He always dressed very nicely. He was able to afford it. My mother's nature was informal, very kind and generous. She always worked very hard. She cooked for my father's employees, two men from Hawaii. My father couldn't find any qualified mechanics in the area, so he hired these two men, who were here alone. She took care of other families' children, and some of them were even married from our house. She was kind of rough in her manners, and she was not pretty in the typical Japanese way. She had deep-set eyes that made Mexican people say 'You look like my mother.' My father wanted us to behave, and do what he said. He came from the era that was militaristic, Meiji era. We had to be very respectful to him because he was sort of typical Japanese Issei – macho, should I say. I was born in Taisho era. Taisho was Emperor for only fifteen years. Showa came after that and lasted sixty years. The last Showa Emperor (Hirohito) died in 1989."

1935: The Marysville Japanese baseball team hosted a game against the visiting Tokyo Giants baseball team, shown here. The Russian sensation, Victor "Star" Starfin, is 5th from the left, standing.

The Tokyo Giants baseball team is one of Molly's bright memories from the Depression years. In March of 1936, the largest crowd ever assembled at the Marysville Municipal Ball Park came to see the Tokyo Giants play the Marysville team that included her older cousin Frank Nakamura. An avid baseball player and fan all his life, Frank also played against the Japanese High School National Champions from Hiroshima, who visited Marysville in 1931. Eleven year-old Molly was captivated by the Giants' star player, Russian-born Victor "Star" Starfin, who was a sensation as the "blue-eyed Japanese". He was one of many Russians who fled to Japan following the 1918 outbreak of the Russian Civil War. "He stood out because he was so tall," she says. Starfin's popularity did not shelter him during World War II. In spite of his status as Japanese baseball's best pitcher during the "dead-ball" era, when many of the country's best players were serving in the Imperial Japanese Army, Starfin was placed in a detention camp with other foreign diplomats and residents. He returned to baseball in 1946.

Molly recalls that after the war, "My girlfriend had a jewelry store on K Street. One of the last surviving players on that team from 1936 came to Sacramento and saw her Japanese store so he stopped in. He told her he wanted to come to Marysville to see the Nakamura Inn, where he stayed when the team was here to play. My uncle owned the inn, and I'm sure that player remembered my aunt's cooking. She was one of the best Japanese cooks in the area. My mother learned a lot from her."

Although Molly says she was sheltered from signs of anti-immigrant sentiment as a young child, she recognizes the gap between her sheltered life and growing anti-Japanese sentiment of the time. Some of the animosity came from Chinese neighbors, who pulled their cars out of her father's garage parking spaces when the Second Sino-Japanese War began in 1937. Asked about the federal government's widely stated fear that Emperor worship, which it called Mikadoism, was being taught at Japanese language schools, Molly recalls: "My girlfriend's father was one of the elders who, whenever there was a new Emperor, would put on white gloves and stand in front of the new Emperor's picture and bow very low. There was a certain way they had to work together to open up the Emperor's portrait. Saikeirei, that's the most formal way of bowing. So my teachers used to say, for respect to the elder or prominent people, the most formal bow is deep down. The next most formal bow was to the middle. I still remember, at the birthday of the Emperor, or New Year's, every time we had a ceremony, everyone went, including all the Japanese language students. Every Japanese community observed it. They thought the Emperor was the god of Japan. Consequently they had to show great respect. As students, we had to do the ceremony for the Emperor or be tapped on the head. It was part of a tradition that went back to feudalistic times."

Many Japanese followed both Buddhist and Shinto practices. Molly says that Shinto traditions, such as bowing to a shrine depicting the Emperor, were to her just another example of the variety of expressions of faith in the Japanese community. "There were thirteen Buddhist denominations before World War II, and Shinto Worship," she says. "For Shrine people, Shinto is a national god image for the country of Japan. There was a story of a goddess who opened that cave and started that shrine. It's a myth to me but they believe it." (Japanese mythology relates the story of Amaterasu, a goddess of the sun and a ruler of heaven, believed to be the legendary ancestor of the current Imperial Family. Offended by the misdeeds of her brother, she came down to earth and hid in a cave. The universe was plunged into pitch darkness and evil thrived, until the gods and goddesses gathered near the cave and lured her out.)

Molly's describes her years at Marysville Union High School: "At public high school, we never assimilated with the other students. You stuck to your same ethnic friends. There was a lot of social dancing for fun. Somehow I was very unsociable in those days. I was always reading and finding new things to do to educate myself. I was always in oratorical contests. I was in CSF, California Scholarship Federation, all the time because my grades were good, mostly A's. Marysville High was about a mile away from my home. We could walk, but we got rides. We didn't want to be out on the road anymore. We always had the feeling that we were not accepted."

June 10, 1942: Marysville Japanese Language High School graduation

Acceptance for Molly and her Japanese friends came in their after school hours, at picnics and social gatherings organized by the Young Buddhists Association. Japanese American students from Placer High School and Yuba City High School joined the Marysville Union High School students in clubs and at games and dances. "We were kept busy all the time," Molly says of these years.

Prejudice from outside the tightly knit Japanese community increased during Molly's high school years, as world events became more ominous. A teen-aged Molly was also feeling the pressure of her family's expectations. "My father told me, 'Of three daughters, you must be the example.' I'm like a second family to my parents, who were thirty-eight and forty when I was born. Helen was fourteen

June 10, 1942: Marysville Japanese Language School Calligraphy Class

years older. My next sister, Katherine, was nine years older. My brother came three years later, and he was always in ill health. I was always kind of in the middle. I became a very abiding child, doing whatever they told me, for the family's sake."

Helen wrote to a university in Kyoto to request admission for Molly. As the "exemplary daughter" she had been groomed to fit in when she arrived. Her Japanese language skills were excellent, though she would learn later that even with years of training her accent marked her in Japan as someone who had spent considerable time in the U.S. She had learned from Helen what the expectations were for young women in Japan. Thanks to her father's courage and persistence, the family had come a long way from the poverty he had experienced in Hiroshima. Much was expected of her. Could she fulfill her father's expectations? Because Molly was so religious, Helen thought she should be in the ministry. How would she fit into Japanese society? Would she be prepared for the rigors of a Japanese university? Any teenage girl would have been wondering about her future.

Welcome party for former Marysville Japanese Language School teacher, Mrs. Chiharu Goda. Molly arranged this large reunion after the war.

The Nakamura family had other worries to occupy them at this time. Joe, never physically strong, contracted diphtheria. "There was a quarantine so we had to move out," Molly recalls. "We stayed with my sister's family for a while. The same doctor who delivered me delivered my brother. Dr. Phillip Hoffman.

25

He was a good family doctor for all the Japanese and he came to help us. I still remember his face. He had a little mole on his cheek." Molly received an injection and she and her father stayed away for a week. Her mother remained behind with Joe, who had a high fever. Molly was fifteen or sixteen years old at the time, and she could see the effect the illness had on her brother. "Joe was interested in sports but wasn't able to do them because of his physical condition. The diphtheria weakened him in his mind and made him depressed. At the age when teenagers go out and make friends he was fearful and had no confidence. My mother always worried."

Joe's diphtheria was not uncommon for those days, but Motoyo had good reason to worry. Diphtheria is a bacterial infection that affects the membranes of the throat and nose. Symptoms include a thick, gray coating on the throat and tonsils, difficulty breathing, bluish skin, chills and fever and a loud, barking cough. It is fatal in about ten percent of cases. More than 150,000 deaths a year were reported when data was first collected in the U.S. in the 1920s. By the time Joe contracted diphtheria, a vaccine was being introduced that reduced the number of cases to nineteen thousand in 1945. Molly does not remember whether Joe received the vaccine, or recovered on his own. What must it have been like for an isolated mother in the 1930s to watch her son struggle with these life-threatening symptoms? If the diphtheria made him weak, Joe was to endure much worse, and soon, under the stress of incarceration.

During her high school years, Molly had progressed enough in her Buddhist studies to help with the Marysville Buddhist Sunday School. As stress in her family's life increased, and concern about a global war mounted, Molly reached a turning point in her life. With encouragement from her mother and Helen, she had attended services and learned about the Pure Land Sect, or Jōdo Shinshu Buddhism. Molly experienced her awakening at age sixteen. She credits this deep religious experience with helping her through the hardships of discrimination and incarceration, and with building a meaningful life.

Even for families long accustomed to anti-Asian sentiment, the tension in 1941 was difficult. Rumors fueled the community's unease. The Nakamuras knew of families in Japan who wrote to warn their American relatives of a coming war, and advised them to return as soon as possible. Through the Young Buddhist Association Molly heard what was happening in Japanese communities throughout Northern California. In spring of 1941, farming families in the Florin area were forced to sell their property to the U.S. Army for expansion of Mather Field, twelve miles southeast of Sacramento. Mather had been closed in 1923, and later served as a quiet subpost of the Presidio U.S. Army Post in San Francisco. It was reestablished as a separate post and activated on May 13, 1941, and expanded from 872 to 4,418 acres the following month. Mather became an important training base and point of embarkation for the Pacific during the war.

Marysville High School's graduating class of 1942 included twelve Japanese American students. Molly says her Caucasian classmates showed more sympathy for the Japanese minority than some of her teachers did. She recalls one painful incident: "In my senior year, 1941-42, I had a teacher who was German. He had changed his name to Slewsalis to sound like he came from somewhere else. He said that in World War I he was incarcerated because he was German. So he told us, 'There's a war coming and you're going to be incarcerated too.'" Long past her eightieth birthday, Molly could feel the sting of those words. "He should have shown us more sympathy. It was cruel for him to say that. I couldn't speak up but I felt it inside. At times we used to feel kind of sad." In the excruciatingly public setting of a high school classroom, Molly and her Japanese American classmates were silent. They were used to being a small, silent minority.

Like most American families, the Nakamuras gathered around the radio to hear the news of the day. They were gathered together on Sunday, December 7, 1941, when news of Pearl Harbor came. Molly recalls that two carpenters from Sacramento were repairing the roof on the house next door, a rental unit her father owned. She ran outside to tell them the news. "They were so surprised," she says. "One man said, 'No, we can't be fighting!' It was so sudden."

For people of Japanese ancestry, freedoms began to disappear quickly in 1942. "Before the war we had a Japanese Association, as other cities did. The presidents of those associations were sent to Santa Fe, so families were separated. My father was a member and donated, but he wasn't head of it. My uncle too, though he was a quiet man." It seems likely that the Nakamura brothers' modesty saved them from the sweeps conducted by the FBI in the days and weeks following Pearl Harbor. Those whom the FBI identified as Issei community leaders were interned in Santa Fe as "enemy aliens" in a prison camp administered by the Justice Department.

The countdown toward incarceration of more than 110,000 people of Japanese ancestry had begun:

On February 14, 1942, the Native Sons of the Golden West called for the eviction of all Japanese Americans, regardless of citizenship status.

On February 15, 1942, Japanese families on Terminal Island near Los Angeles were the first ordered to relocate. Three hundred families left voluntarily; the remaining two hundred were given one month to leave. Ten days later they were ordered to leave within fifty-seven hours.

On February 19, 1942, President Franklin D. Roosevelt issued Executive Order 9066, giving Secretary of War Henry L. Stimson the authority to remove the Japanese and their American-born children from places designated as military areas.

On March 2, 1942, Lt. General John L. DeWitt exercised his authority under Executive Order 9066 for the first time, issuing Pubic Proclamation Number 1. It created Military District No. 1, which included the western half of California, Oregon and Washington, and part of southern Arizona. Military District No. 2 comprised the rest of all four states.

On March 18, 1942, President Roosevelt issued Executive Order 9102 creating the War Relocation Authority (WRA), a non-military agency with authority to formulate and carry out a program for relocation of persons evacuated from Military Districts. Milton S. Eisenhower was appointed director.

On March 21, 1942, Congress passed a law setting the punishment for disobeying Army orders at one year in prison and a fine of $5,000 — more than a year's salary for most people.

On March 27, 1942, Lt. General DeWitt issued Proclamation No. 4, forbidding all people of Japanese ancestry from moving. People with as little as one-sixteenth Japanese blood (one Japanese great, great grandparent) were included in this group.

On March 28, 1942, the federal government imposed an eight p.m. curfew on all people of Japanese ancestry.

On May 12, 1942, Exclusion Order 69, affecting Japanese residents of Marysville, was issued. Japanese residents west of Highway 99, also known as D Street, were ordered to go to an assembly center. Failure to comply with curfew or exclusion orders was subject to criminal penalties.

On May 17, 1942, Civilian Exclusion orders for the Sacramento area were issued from the Headquarters Western Defense Command and Fourth Army, Presidio of San Francisco, California. The orders said, "...all persons of Japanese ancestry, both alien and non-alien, [will] be excluded from that portion of Military Area No. 1 described as follows: All of the City of Sacramento, State of California."

On May 27, 1942, the WRA opened the Tule Lake relocation center.

By August 7, 1942, the evacuation of 110,000 persons of Japanese ancestry from their homes in Military District No. 1 and the California portion of Military District No. 2 was complete.

The Arboga Detention Center, also called the Marysville Detention Center, was a former migrant worker camp about eight miles south of town. Construction on the Arboga barracks began on March 27. Although the facility's one hundred sixty buildings were ready for occupancy by April 16, heavy rains turned roads to mud, delaying occupancy until May 8. "It was such a last minute order from the

28

President that they didn't have time to build the barracks, so people had to wait," Molly recalls. About a hundred Marysville residents living west of Highway 99 were interned in the Arboga center. Other occupants came from Placer and Sacramento Counties, more than two thousand four hundred in all. They lived in the Arboga barracks until June 29, a total of fifty-three days, before being relocated to Camp Amache in Colorado. Today only a small marker shows the site ever existed.

Molly and her family lived within a two-block radius east of Highway 99, designated a "free zone" because the eastern side of the highway was further away – if only by a few hundred feet – from the Pacific Ocean. In the "free zone," Japanese were allowed to stay in their homes while waiting for internment, rather than having to report to an assembly center, but they were not allowed to travel further than five blocks from their homes. "They were afraid the Japanese navy would come and Japanese Americans would be spies. It's just that they were scared," Molly says. She recalls that before the March 27 travel restrictions were imposed, one of her classmates left the west coast. Some Bay Area families, including those of student and faculty members from the University of California at Berkeley, moved to Marysville to avoid being moved to the Tanforan Assembly Center in San Bruno. Tanforan was the second largest assembly center of the seventeen established by the U.S. Army. It was a horseracing track, and barracks were made from horse stalls and temporary buildings on the track. Open from April 28 to October 13, 1942, it held nearly eight thousand people.

In spite of disruption all around her, Molly was able to finish her high school course work. Marysville Union High School held its graduation ceremony on June 10, 1942. Molly had looked forward to that day. Her best friend Melba Kaminaka was class valedictorian. They were proud of her accomplishment, which was especially noteworthy when fear was increasing among Japanese Americans. They made plans to celebrate. All of that came to a stop when the house detention order was imposed in May. "With the curfew we could not attend the ceremony," Molly says. She and Melba received their diplomas by mail. In Melba's place, Mary Ann Dunn, later a teacher in North Sacramento, became the new class valedictorian. It was an ongoing source of sadness on both sides. Molly says, "After the war Mary Ann would tell us how sorry she was she got to do the speech instead. I told her, 'Don't be sorry. I've accepted that.'"

It seemed to the isolated Japanese community that anything could happen. Rumors mounted that all people of Japanese ancestry would be rounded up, put on ships and forced to go to Japan. Even American born Japanese, who were U.S. citizens, would have to go. When it became clear that Japanese people would be imprisoned, Nobujiro began selling off the inventory in his appliance store in Sacramento. Opportunists descended on Sacramento's Japantown to take advantage of the businesses' plight. The WRA published a list of warehouses it would contract to store belongings, as well as agents who were authorized to take control of Japanese people's property. Many Japanese were distrustful of the government and chose instead to store furniture and personal property with friends, or in basements. The Nakamuras sold off the furniture in their home. Nobujiro had to sign over control of his properties: the house and garage in Marysville and a commercial building at Third and C Streets in Sacramento. He had no way of knowing how long this arrangement would last, or whether he would be able to get his property back in the future. But it was the best he could do to protect what he had worked so hard to gain. It seems unlikely that a businessman of his caliber would have left such a monumental decision to the blind luck of a WRA list. Molly does not know the name of the agent he entrusted, but whatever went into the decision, Nobujiro had chosen well. The agent collected rent from his properties and mailed it to Nobujuro while the family was interned.

Molly recalls the day when her family received its notice to relocate: "When the notice came we were issued tags with numbers that identified us. My family's number was 39312. We were given a box, like a chest, with that number on it. We were to bring only what we could carry with us, and that box. I think Japanese people today should know." Molly does not recall the contents of her box that day, but remembers that somehow she was able to hold onto her biwa. And she remembers the date. On July 14, 1942, the Nakamuras and all remaining Japanese American families were loaded into railroad cars on a site near what is now known as Washington Square in Marysville. As armed guards watched, "They put about one hundred of us on the train at seven in the evening," Molly says. "They didn't tell us where we were going. They pulled the shades down so we couldn't see out. There were armed guards on the train with us. The first time we saw anything was Mount Shasta the next morning. I had never been that far north before. I remember it was snow-capped, even in July, like Mount Fuji. It was beautiful."

Native Americans revere Shasta as a sacred space, but to Molly and her family at that moment, it was a symbol of how far they were from home and anything like their old familiar lives.

CHAPTER THREE

Life at Camp

The train pulled to a stop in a field near present-day Newell, California. Molly's brother in law, George Iwasaki, had arrived a few weeks earlier as part of an advance team to set up medical facilities. His job as a pharmacist gave him access to the use of an automobile, and he arranged for a car to pick up the Nakamuras at the train track, saving them the truck ride. In the process, the Nakamuras were separated from the Marysville neighbors they had ridden with on the train. The car took them to units occupied by families from Placer County, where they filled in an unoccupied space, and met the people who would share their walls, bathrooms, laundry facilities, meals – and lives – for the next three years.

Aerial view of Tule Lake Relocation Center showing Abalone Mountain. The creator of this photograph, taken between 1941-1945, is unknown. Contributing institution: California State University Sacramento.

The northwest corner of Modoc County, at an altitude of four thousand feet, is some of the least hospitable land in the West. In this vicinity the Modoc Nation made its last stand against the U.S. Army in 1873. The Lava Beds National Monument, about forty-five minutes south of Tule Lake, is so rugged that it allowed the Modoc to hold defensive positions against heavily armed cavalry for several months. One internee described the area as "a treeless wasteland" where winter snowstorms alternated with sandstorms, and no flowers bloomed in the dry desert-like climate and volcanic soil. The Japanese words for Tule Lake consisted of three kanji characters: Crane, Mountain Range and Lake. The internees named the mountains that marked the camp's boundaries: Castle Rock marked the entrance to the camp, situated at the bottom of a dry lakebed; Abalone Mountain rose behind it. In fall, the sky was alive with thousands of geese and ducks joining the great migration in the Pacific Flyway.

These are high desert conditions. Weather at Tule Lake ranges from the negative numbers in winter to the eighties in summer. The growing season for crops is very short – about eighty days. Wind is always a factor. On the flat lakebed, even light rain made mud holes of the unpaved streets. The internees had never heard of Tule Lake, and the mild climate of the Sacramento Valley had not prepared them for the harsh winter ahead.

Molly and her family arrived in July. "When we reached Tule Lake, there was an iron gate with a tower. We were assigned to a barrack that was already mostly full, mainly with Placer County people, mostly farmers. They were nice and kind. The Yamasaki family, who had had a big nursery, occupied two units in our barrack. Kimi Mizusaki, my mother's niece, had one family unit; the Ohara family had the other unit. My family was assigned to Block 43, Barrack 05, so our address was 4305C. The arrangement of the camp, we later found out, was twelve to fourteen barracks to a block. A ditch surrounded each block. Our block was near the stockade. All of us, my mother, father, brother and I, were assigned to live together in a unit, which was a single room. My sister Helen, because she was married, was assigned to a separate barrack with her husband and daughter, in a block near the hospital. My sister Katherine and Uncle Buntaro and his family lived in the next block with Marysville residents, Block 48. My mother used to say, 'Always together,' and even though we were in different blocks, we were all at Tule Lake together."

At its peak population, eighteen thousand seven hundred people were imprisoned at Tule Lake. They lived in barracks hastily built in 1942. Each barrack measured twenty by one hundred feet, and was divided into five units of about five hundred square feet each. One family was assigned to each unit, or units, depending on family size. Each block contained thirteen or fourteen family barracks and communal areas for groups of two hundred fifty to three hundred people, with a mess hall, a laundry building/boiler room and a small ironing room. One empty barrack could be used as a church, store, school or community hall, depending on the needs of the inmates of the block. Rooms were equipped with one light bulb, a coal-burning heat stove, and metal Army cots and blankets.

There was no other furniture, and no partitions. Two latrine/shower buildings, one for women and another for men, were located in the center of the block. There was always a line of people waiting to use the facilities. Many internees have described the lack of privacy. "For me the worst part of barracks life was the group bathroom," Molly says. "There were no curtains or walls on the shower stalls or the toilets. It was open and everybody could watch you. No privacy, but we had to take showers, that's all." The indignity remained with her for a lifetime. "To this day I don't want to take a shower; I'd rather have a tub. I didn't even learn how to use my shower when we renovated our bathroom at home."

Prisoners provided the labor to operate the camps, which were intended to be self-sufficient. Inmates did all the work of sustaining the incarcerated: they ran the mess halls, grew crops, taught school children, organized church activities and baseball games, staffed the camp newspaper, ran the co-op stores and took on construction projects such as raised walkways over the mud. Doctors and other professionals in the camp were paid nineteen dollars a month, the highest salary an inmate could earn. Nonprofessionals were paid sixteen dollars a month and apprentices or part-timers twelve dollars a month.

The Army provided food limited to the cost of a soldier's rations, from forty-seven to as little as thirty-five cents per person per day. Meals were served at long rows of tables in large mess halls. "The breakfast wasn't bad," Molly recalls, "But for three years we were fed smelly mutton stew nearly every day. Even now I have never acquired a taste for lamb or mutton. My daughter says, 'Mother you're so choosy,' but I hate it. They had dried fish after awhile, cooked in soy sauce or fried or something. The incarcerated people raised vegetables for the camp. We didn't have a lot of them, but some. Other foods came from the Klamath Falls area."

For more than a year, Nobujiro refused to eat any meal but breakfast in the mess hall. Motoyo brought him rice, and prepared whatever she could on two hot plates in the family unit. "Not from the beginning but during the last year and a half, the camp had a store, they called it a canteen, and it sold fish, meat and vegetables," Molly says. Funds began arriving from the rents on Nobujiro's properties. Motoyo used them to shop at the canteen every day.

The familiar food was more than just an alternative to the monotonous mess hall fare. It offered some measure of control over basic decisions. Although he fared better than many in his generation, incarceration was hard on Nobujiro. He was still the head of the family, but he was no longer a businessman, nor an influential community leader. Molly noticed the changes. "In camp he couldn't wear a suit because everyone would stare at him, so he wore a sweater. He never had anything like that before." Government policy prohibited Issei from taking any leadership role in the camps. He spoke very little English, and like many

Tule Lake Recreation Dept. staff. Some of the people pictured include: seated 1st Row: Mrs. Tsumura; Ms. Hosokawa, Director; Nobuko Tsuchida, Ikebana teacher; Hatsuyo Oda, crepe paper flower instructor. 2nd Row: Tamotsu Kataoka, sewing teacher; Sumiye Noguchi, tea ceremony teacher. 3rd Row: (third from left) Nobujiro Nakamura, Molly's father, repaired sewing machines.

Issei, he found himself having to depend on the younger generation for basic communication. Molly recalls that he found some purpose, and some recognition, repairing Singer sewing machines for busy seamstresses in the camp sewing classes, and spending time with other Issei men. "They all got together, the old citizens like my father," Molly says. "There was a lot of socializing, and marriages being arranged. My father took some rings with him, and he sold them in camp. Even there, my father enjoyed business."

Small improvements that arrived courtesy of Nobujiro's pre-war business enterprises made life more bearable. "We were allowed to bring in some of the appliances my father sold," Molly recalls. "A Maytag washer and dryer and a small refrigerator that was another brand, like GE. The War Relocation Authority shipped them for free. Everybody came to our unit to use them."

For the younger generation, adapting to the limitations of incarceration was a challenge they took pride in meeting. "I guess I must have learned from my father about making the best of what was available. I had a younger friend (Hiroko Tsuda) who told me, 'Molly, when you started teaching me craft work, you taught me how to eat tomato and cucumber with mayonnaise and salt on top, a tomato and cucumber sandwich.' I must have learned this from my father when there was no meat in the camp. I served it to my Sunday school children. In camp we accepted everything that was served to us, to survive. Farmers grew Japanese vegetables like daikon radish in Tule Lake. They brought them to the mess hall. It was kind of fun seeing two hundred of us eating all at the same time. There was a fixed time you could eat. We never had a line. It was all assigned. We would go in early and sit down and they would serve us."

On the Abalone Mountain side of camp, women ventured out in groups to dig up small shells from the dry lakebed. They painted the shells with fingernail polish, and made corsages, jewelry, picture frames and anything else they could think of. Molly recalls the hobbies that occupied her mother's generation: "After all, they didn't have to cook anymore, so they had time. I used to see a lot of people making shell jewelry. My mother did too. She also learned Japanese doll making." The dolls Motoyo produced in camp have held a treasured place in Molly's home for more than sixty years.

While she did enjoy the company of other Issei women, Motoyo spent many of her days caring for and worrying about Joe, whose health continued to be delicate. During incarceration he was diagnosed with pleurisy, a painful infection of the lining of the lungs. It seems possible that he was also showing symptoms of the tuberculosis that was diagnosed after the war. American born boys in the camp had varying reactions to incarceration. "My brother did not accept the situation," Molly says. "He was weakened in body and spirit. He attended the Tule Lake camp high school. The boys played a lot of sports, like baseball, but because of his health he still could not join in. He was too young to have a job. He was often depressed, and the climate and living conditions of the camp did not help. My mother worried about his health all the time." No reassurance was to come from the camp doctor. Medical facilities at Tule Lake were short on medicine, doctors and nurses. The chief physician, Reese Pedicord, referred to Japanese American patients, nurses and staff doctors as "yellow-bellies" and "Japs."

The winter of 1943 was especially hard. January snowfall was four to five times the level of other winters, and the temperature fell to minus four degrees. The green, unseasoned wood used in barracks construction dried and shrank, leaving large cracks where wind blew the cold and sand through floors, walls and roofs. "We had one tall, round coal stove in the center of our unit," Molly says.

"Military trucks dropped coal in a space outside the boiler room. Everybody went and shoveled coal into a bucket. Coal dust was everywhere. Tule Lake was cold. I remember it snowing in June." Adults in the camp received a clothing allowance of three dollars and seventy-five cents a month. Fortunately, the family brought enough cash with them to order winter coats from the Montgomery Ward catalog. "They gave us army cots and blankets because we didn't bring enough. We didn't know it was going to be that cold." Molly says

For those who were young and in good health, the weather made everything more difficult, but life went on. Molly's cousin, Frank Nakamura, was manager of the camp records office. He and his wife Hatsue had a son, Gary, born in Tule Lake in 1942. Molly took a full time job in the recreation department office at sixteen dollars a month, but swapped it for a part time job in the mess hall and used the extra time to study and learn. "I had to work only a couple of hours, then I was free to go to classes. We didn't know how long we would be incarcerated. It was … come to think of it, we would always wonder when the war was going to end." Molly responded to that uncertainty by plunging into what she describes as the equivalent of a college education through a deep immersion in Japanese culture. "It was the unpopular thing to do for many of my generation in the camp," she says.

Her teachers were some of the finest Buddhist scholars in the Western hemisphere. A proposal to incarcerate all Japanese people in Hawaii was vetoed by Hawaiian businessmen, who depended on their labor. As a compromise, prominent Japanese leaders, including Buddhist priests, were rounded up and

sent to camps on the mainland. "We had so many Buddhist and Christian ministers from the island of Hawaii. They used to start giving sermons at six o'clock in the morning. We used to walk about a mile to different recreation halls to attend services. There was a ditch and beyond that was a unit built for the Hawaiian ministers. Their families joined them after two years. It was on the north side and we called it 'Alaska Unit' because it was so far north."

With her friend Sunaye Sakamoto, Molly set up a Dharma Sunday School. It provided some continuity in her life, a link to her pre-war work helping with the Marysville Buddhist Sunday School. She taught every Sunday at Tule Lake. The ward recreation hall was used on weekends for meetings, classrooms and church. Recreational class supplies were ordered

Molly and her best friend in Tule Lake, Sunaye Takagi Sakamoto

December 13, 1945: Molly and friends at Tule Lake

from the Montgomery Ward catalog. Molly and Sunaye taught their young charges embroidery, ordering floss from the catalog.

Though Molly's study of biwa was cut short when her teacher was interned at Heart Mountain, Wyoming, she performed in pro—grams featuring both Japanese and Western cultural offerings almost every weekend. She studied *mizuhiki*, an ancient Japanese art using a special cord made of rice paper, tightly wound, starched and colored, and then made into decorations given away at important occasions. *Mizuhiki* was traditionally used to tie the hair of the samurai.

Her studies also included classes in Chinese and Japanese calligraphy. The WRA shipped materials from New York to set up a formal tea ceremony room for lessons. Mrs. Sumiye Noguchi conducted the tea ceremony lesson using equipment the WRA shipped from her home in Sacramento. Molly continued the Ikebana lessons she had begun as a twelve year-old. Mrs. Jack Tsuchida, whose

1945: Molly, second from left, best friend Sunaye Sakamoto on the far left and Jane Nakano Tochiura on the right

husband was a former president of a Hiroshima Society group, taught classes in the Ikenobo School of Ikebana. Floral materials were virtually nonexistent, so students had to be creative. Flowers came from a class on crepe paper flower making. Sagebrush was the major source of greenery.

Other classes were doll making, sewing and cooking. A teacher from San Francisco taught classes in Japanese etiquette. "I learned how to cook in Tule Lake," Molly says. "There were always so many people around helping my mother that I didn't learn at home. Our teacher in the camp was an expert. He must have been a chef. I went to his demonstrations in the mess hall with my sister. I don't know how he got the ingredients. We learned to make sushi, and *kamaboko* (fish cake) from scratch using a special kind of fish, and soup stock from bonito. In those days the bonito was dried into a hard brick and you shaved it and added cornstarch and water. My sister and I would grind the mixture in a bowl for at least half an hour. The instructor handed out his recipes on a mimeographed sheet. I kept them for many years. All our books were mimeographed and held together with twine.

"In Tule Lake I studied the geography of Japan, including transportation and communication. Taiwan was in that book because it was still a territory of Japan. I did that for almost two years. I also took a course on morality, *shushin*, that was taught in Japan. It was designed to discipline children to be kind to living things, from your parents, to your animals."

Radios were not allowed in camp, though a few were smuggled in. Rumors circulated that Japan was actually winning the war. Hot tempers fueled by anger, despair and anxiety were part of camp life. So were attempts to get around the

Tule Lake Japanese Language School students.

WRA's rules. Both Japanese prisoners and Caucasian captors engaged in hoarding supplies. The administration acknowledged that many internees went hungry and cooks were short on food, in spite of what it described as "generous" food budget. Molly says, "In each mess hall there was a chef. One man was always in charge of food items that military trucks delivered. For a while, one man was hoarding some of the rice and fruits that were to be fed to the two hundred people in our block. He was using the rice to make sake to sell. In his unit he had a space near the ceiling, covered with a canvas tarp. The military police came and raided the unit where the stolen goods were hidden. I had a cold that day, so I was home and I saw the raid. They slashed the ceiling, and rice and apples came pouring out. Then they arrested the chef. But they couldn't do anything and the chef came back and announced, 'I am free, I wasn't investigated for anything.' People just laughed, you know. The chef and this man from San Francisco and one of my relatives were involved. In another incident, a man from Sacramento was assassinated because people thought he was doing business with the WRA, making money. They don't know who killed him. People who worked with the government were called *inu*, dogs."

Molly vividly remembers the loyalty review program implemented in 1943. The War Department began to reclassify Japanese Americans from 4-C "enemy alien" to 1-A so that Nisei would be eligible to serve in the U.S. military.

Most of the teachers came from Hawaii.

Sunday School Teachers
with Rev. Ono, Ward V
Tule Lake.

Tule Lake Japanese
language class, high
school level; Teacher
Rev. Takezono, from
Hilo, Hawaii. Hiroshi
Kashiwagi, standing,
5th from the left.

Bottom row, 3rd from
Left: Ikebana teacher,
Mrs. Nobuko Tsuchida
with instructors.

Tule Lake Relocation Center Omote Tea Ceremony class. The WRA purchased
tea room furnishings from a New York store. Instructor, Mrs. S. Noguchi.

November 1945: Ward V, Young Buddhist Association convention. Many teachers and reverends were from Hawaii.

1944: WRA recreation and sports department staff.

October 6, 1844: Students in Ikenobo Ikebana and mizuhiki classes

A questionnaire was developed to identify potential volunteers. The WRA decided to use the same questionnaire to identify inmates who might be released from captivity early. All adults were required to fill out a form entitled "Application for Leave Clearance," later titled "Information for Leave Clearance." Questions 27 and 28 on the questionnaire caused divisions within families and between internees, and led to a crisis throughout the system of camps. The questions were:

"27: Are you willing to serve in the armed forces of the United States on combat duty, wherever ordered?

28: Will you swear unqualified allegiance to the United States of America and faithfully defend the United States from any and all attack by foreign or domestic forces, and forswear any form of allegiance or obedience to the Japanese emperor, or any other foreign government, power or organization?"

The wording of the questions generated mistrust and confusion. For the Nisei, would saying "yes" to the first question mean they were volunteering for military service? The Issei especially didn't want to answer no to the second question, because they were not allowed to become U.S. citizens. If they said they were not Japanese either, they would have had no country. But would saying yes imply that they had, at some time, been loyal to the emperor? Prisoners at other camps were allowed time to discuss the questionnaire at workshops where their questions were answered. Responses at those camps were generally positive. At Tule Lake, information on the loyalty registration program came late, leaving inmates little time to think about the implications of their answers. Making matters worse, the loyalty registration form was printed only in English.

Males of an eligible age for military service who answered no to both questions were known as No-No Boys. Tule Lake had the largest number of inmates whose answers categorized them as "disloyal." The Tule Lake Committee, which

1944: Tule Lake Buddhist Church Ward V Sunday School students and teachers.

preserves the history of the camp and provides education on the incarceration experience, notes that the Army had hoped to recruit 3,500 men from the WRA camps to serve in a segregated all-Nisei combat unit. Only 1,181 volunteered, and only fifty-seven of those were from Tule Lake. Many Nisei had volunteered or enlisted in the military before 1942, but were discharged after Pearl Harbor or reclassified as 4-C, "enemy aliens." Now they and their families were locked up indefinitely. Many wondered why they should volunteer.

On July 31, 1943 the Tule Lake Relocation Center was designated the Segregation Center for "disloyal" evacuees from all ten relocation camps throughout the U.S. Relocation of about twelve thousand "disloyals" and their family members to Tule Lake began immediately, and was completed by October 11. The WRA added a thousand military police to increase security at the Tule Lake Segregation Center. Tanks rolled in and an eight-foot double "man-proof" fence was constructed to create maximum security. An open field in front of the jail was the site of the stockade. Fenced with barbed wire and surrounded by guard towers equipped with sweeping floodlights, it was patrolled by soldiers armed with submachine guns. Mass demonstrations began in Tule Lake on November 1, 1943. The Army took control of Tule Lake and did not hand it back over to the WRA until January 14, 1944.

In Block 42, near the Nakamuras, several dozen men refused to fill out the loyalty questionnaire. All were imprisoned in county jails in Klamath Falls and Alturas. They were removed from jail after a week without being charged with a crime, and taken to Camp Tulelake, a former Civilian Conservation Corps camp near the concentration camp site. More than a hundred protesters were indefinitely jailed for disobeying the command to answer the loyalty questions. No one was ever charged with a crime. When asked what she saw of the violence and turmoil at Tule Lake, Molly says, "I saw all of that. I witnessed it."

The Renunciation Act of 1944 again required Japanese Americans to state their loyalty in writing. Prior to the law's passage, U.S. citizenship could be lost only by conviction for treason; the Renunciation Act allowed people to renounce citizenship when the country was in a state of war by making a declaration to the Attorney General. The intention of the Act was to encourage Japanese American internees to renounce citizenship so that they could be deported to Japan. Scholars of the mass internment have made the case that the Act was a strategy to continue detaining Japanese Americans not accused of any wrongdoing once the exclusion order was rescinded. Even Tule Lake Project Director Raymond R. Best wrote of the confusion and turmoil created by the government's representation to internees that their choices were renunciation, in which case they could stay in the camp with their families, or forced relocation into a hostile population and separation from their families. Of the 5,589 Japanese Americans who renounced their U.S. citizenship, 5,461 were detained at Tule Lake, where seventy-three percent of families had at least one member who gave up their citizenship. Of that group, 1,327 of them, including young children, were expatriated to Japan.

One of the renunciants was Molly's brother Joe. "He was about sixteen at the time, and maybe that was why he didn't hear more about it. If he had been eighteen, he would have faced imprisonment in the segregation jail. Conditions there were terrible. My mother was sure that he would not survive there," Molly says. Photos have documented stockade guards beating prisoners, some of whom were reported to have been minors.

Another renunciant was Molly's classmate in the Tule Lake Japanese language school, Sacramento-born, Placer County resident Hiroshi Kashiwagi. Already designated a No-No Boy for his answers on the loyalty questionnaire, he and his family had been ostracized by the Japanese American community. Civil rights attorney Wayne Collins, born in Sacramento and educated in San Francisco, was a co-founder and director of the Northern California American Civil Liberties Union. An ardent fighter for the rights of Japanese American citizens, he filed class action suits after the war on behalf of thousands of internees who were deceived or coerced into renouncing their citizenship. His clients included Hiroshi Kashiwagi, whose citizenship was restored in 1959 when a federal court recognized that his renunciation was made under duress. He became a playwright, author and actor, and is considered a pioneer of Asian American theater.

In 1948, U.S. District Louis Judge Goodman included these remarks in his opinion concerning cases involving renunciation at Tule Lake: [Giving up their U.S. citizenship was] "the outgrowth of the combined experience of evacuation, loss of home, isolation from outside communication and concentration in an enclosed, guarded, overpopulated camp with little occupation, inadequate and uncomfortable living accommodations, dreary and unhealthful surroundings and climatic conditions – producing neuroses built on fear, anxiety, resentment, uncertainty, hopelessness and despair of eventual rehabilitation."

Molly says of this time: "As a woman, filling out the form was voluntary for me. I didn't fill it out; I stayed neutral. We were supposed to declare whether we wished to renounce our citizenship, or to stay in the U.S."

Molly had less sympathy for some of her other relatives who chose not to sign the loyalty oath. "My second cousins were in the Jerome, Arkansas relocation camp. They wanted to be expatriated. They were in the group of radicals moved from Jerome to Tule Lake. Many of those Japanese didn't know where Japan was. They marched around the camp with the scarves on their head. They had ministers who told them Japan was winning the war. When the camp closed down, because he had been educated in an American high school, my cousin went to work for [General] MacArthur after the war."

To make room for the new inmates, the WRA allowed those deemed loyal to relocate away from the "military zone" to the Midwest, south and east coast. Molly's autograph book, handmade in camp, records some of the poignant farewells of departing internees who chose to relocate. Many included their barrack number with their signature. Some added a reference to where they had come from, or where they hoped to find a new place to live.

> August 13, 1943:
> Dear Molly, When you're outside and resettled, do think of me sometimes.
> Ayako Kumamoto

> Sept. 12, 1943: ... Upon relocation, I wish you all the luck, happiness and success in the line of Buddhism. ... Cheeko Ishida, #58, Kirkland Wash.

> November 11, 1945: ... As the autumn leaves are swept before the gust of wind, so have we been swept along with the rush of events. Trying times are soon forgotten, but pleasant memories of friends, the carefree center life, the Sunday services, the thought of having been a co-Sunday school teacher with you – all these memories will live fondly on. Sincerely, Kimi Kodani

> August 12, 1943, Tulelake W.R.A: To Molly: I would like to remember you as the fine "Biwa" singer. Your voice is full of joy which will be the inspiration ... Kenneth B. Yasuda

Photo by Dennis Spear

The riots, marches and protests, the daily humiliations and sad tales of broken families, Molly leaves to others to tell. In the end, she says, "My family stayed neutral, and we didn't want to move to a different camp." Before the war, Molly had dual Japanese and American citizenship. As a result of the anxiety over loyalty oaths and renunciations in camp, her father wrote to the Japanese Embassy after the war, revoking her Japanese citizenship. Those who chose to stay in Tule Lake, as Molly and her parents did, were interviewed by the WRA to determine their loyalty to the U.S. Molly recalls that after she was deemed "not disloyal" the WRA allowed her to take a bus to Klamath Falls to go shopping. "The trip was offered on three occasions. I went twice. It was a half day trip," she says. "You had to sign up. Everybody wanted to get out. It was a treat for us. Imagine if you were confined in one place for three years and never saw anything but your army barracks. The WRA issued us rationing coupons. I remember I bought nylons and sugar," she says. "It was so nice to get out of the place. I will never forget that feeling."

The population at Tule Lake Segregation Center was the largest of the ten internment camps nationwide. More than eighteen thousand seven hundred people crowded into a camp built for fifteen thousand. When Tule Lake became a segregation center, those deemed "loyal" were offered the chance to move away from the West Coast. Buntaro chose to move his family to the internment camp at Amache, Colorado. For most internees, the pull of family and the familiar were too great, and they chose to stay as close as possible. Molly recalls this story about how unfamiliar people on the east coast were with Asian immigrants: "During the wartime, Japanese Americans settled in the New York area. I heard about one woman who was pregnant and had a baby. All Japanese when they are born have a temporary bluish black spot on their backs. The doctors didn't have any experience with that. The spot is about four inches in diameter, and it fades away. Some of the doctors thought it was some kind of birthmark, but they didn't know what it was."

Today, it seems like a great irony that "I could have gone outside the camp for an education, like my girlfriend Melba Kaminaka," Molly says. "She and another girl, June Hiraoka, who was a couple of years older, went out from Tule Lake to become cadet nurses, and they were able to work in New York. Melba never got married, and she became the head surgical nurse at Sutter General Hospital in Sacramento. She was the one who was supposed to be give the valedictory speech for my high school class." Molly never considered leaving her parents, who could speak no English, and her brother, whose health was never to recover.

If they had been willing to split up, the Nakamura family could have avoided internment altogether. The minister at the Marysville Buddhist church was transferred to a church in Salt Lake City. Molly recalls: "He invited my father to move to Salt Lake City, which was a free zone, rather than face internment. But it was a long journey and my father thought he would rather keep the family together. My sister Helen was already married and had family. He wanted us all to face internment together. He said he thought it might be safer to be incarcerated, because we heard about incidences of Japanese people being hurt." Keeping his extended family together through incarceration may have helped everyone, especially Nobujiro as head of the family. Although the times to come were difficult, the Nakamuras were to fare better than many families did once they were allowed to leave.

Asked how her life might be different if she had not been interned, Molly says she has not spent much time thinking about it. "I would have done what my parents told me to do. I don't think you'll find that kind of daughter now. It's a different generation with a different environment. They have not gone through discrimination. They are accepted as Americans like other ethnic groups." She pauses for a few seconds, perhaps thinking of her visits to Hiroshima and the family members she has met there. "If my parents had stayed in Hiroshima, maybe I would have been killed in the bombing. "

The term "concentration camp" to describe the Japanese internment gained greater use after a 1998 exhibit at Ellis Island. The Japanese American National Museum and the American Jewish Committee issued a joint statement that read:

> "A concentration camp is a place where people are imprisoned not because of any crimes they have committed, but simply because of who they are ... Despite differences [in the nature of concentration camps around the world], all had one thing in common: the people in power removed a minority group from the general population and the rest of society let it happen."

The Japanese American Citizens League has ratified the *Power of Words Handbook*, which has this to say: "... many euphemisms have been used to describe the experiences of Japanese Americans who were forced from their homes and communities during World War II. Words like *evacuation, relocation, and assembly centers* imply that the United States Government was trying to rescue Japanese Americans from a disastrous environment on the West Coast and simply help them move to a new gathering place. These terms strategically mask the fact that thousands of Japanese Americans were denied their rights as U.S. citizens, and forcibly ordered to live in poorly constructed barracks on sites that were surrounded by barbed wire and guard towers. Although the use of euphemisms was commonplace during World War II, and in many subsequent years, we realize that the continued use of these inaccurate terms is highly problematic."

The site of the relocation center was designated a national monument in 2008, and is now part of the National Parks Service. It is known as the Tule Lake Unit of WWII Valor in the Pacific National Monument. A plaque memorializing the site as a state historical landmark reads: "Tule Lake was one of ten American concentration camps established during World War II to incarcerate 110,000 persons of Japanese ancestry, of whom the majority were American citizens, behind barbed wire and guard towers without charge, trial or establishment of guilt. These camps are reminders of how racism, economic and political exploitation, and expediency can undermine the constitutional guarantees of United States citizens and aliens alike. May the injustices and humiliation suffered here never recur."

Molly has this to say:
"I call it relocation. There are some young Japanese Americans now who say they should be called concentration, not relocation, camps. I could care less whether they are called relocation or concentration. I don't need to worry about that. I remember it. People have sympathy for us. I tell them the past is past. We have to look forward to live."

In 1953, on their honeymoon drive from Sacramento to Victoria, British Columbia, Molly and her new husband, Kazuo Kimura, stopped off to see what was left of the Tule Lake Relocation Center. Although she has attended every reunion of her Marysville Union High School class, and the Tule Lake reunion events held in Sacramento every five years since 1960, she has never gone on the pilgrimage trips organized by detainees of Tule Lake. She and her best camp friend from Hawaii still exchange gifts, California persimmons and Kona coffee. The last reunion event she attended, at a Sacramento hotel, was in 1998.

The National Park Service has embarked on a General Management Plan effort to determine how the Tule Lake site will be managed in the future. The Park Service notes: "The unit offers a compelling venue for engaging in a dialogue concerning racism and discrimination, war hysteria, failure of political leadership, and the fragility of democracy in times of crisis."

ENTRIES FROM MOLLY'S TULE LAKE DIARY
(translated from the Japanese)

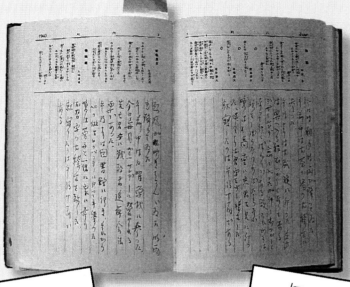

Photo by Dennis Spear

January 1, 1945

Today is much-awaited New Year's Day 1945. This is the third time we have observed New Year's in Tule Lake under incarceration with our two countries at war. It was warm early spring weather all day. All the residents of our Block 43 gathered in the mess hall and we had a program, a solemn service. Mr. Okazaki was the chairman. All day long, people came to our home to exchange New Year's greetings. In the afternoon our family went around offering greetings for the New Year's and visiting. At night I crocheted. My New Year's resolution is to study the Japanese language harder and not neglect my studies. Second, to write in my diary. I went to bed at 10 p.m.

April 12, 1945

Today we had icicles and lots of mist. I reviewed my Japanese language class work. In the afternoon I went to sewing school. All the people of the world were shocked to hear of the sudden death of President Roosevelt. At night I went to school and had a civics lesson, and shushin, morality lesson (appreciation of parents, country, community).

January 3, 1945

This morning we see thick fog. All the roofs of the barracks had icicles hanging. The mess hall staff began working today. (New Year's was observed for five days.) I woke up at 6 a.m. to help at the mess hall. My Japanese language school is still observing holidays. I was very busy with many activities during holidays and I neglected my studies, so in the afternoon I resumed my study. In between, I crocheted. At nighttime we went to meet my father's good friend Mr. Fujita, who was ill, and to exchange New Year's greetings. Despite our inconvenient and unsatisfying life, today I had a healthy and safe day. It is important to think positively and appreciate that Amida Buddha is always protecting us and giving us strength.

CHAPTER FOUR

Starting Over

Nearly one hundred thousand people were killed outright on August 6, 1945, when the U.S. dropped an atomic bomb on Hiroshima City. Nearly seventy-four thousand people died on August 9 when the U.S. dropped a plutonium bomb on Nagasaki. The Empire of Japan signed surrender documents on September 2. A few days later, the Nakamura family received orders to evacuate the Tule Lake camp. Rumors still circulated that news accounts of the bombings and the surrender were false, and that Japanese ships were on their way to pick up the internees and return them to the homeland. But the Nakamuras were ready to accept the evidence, heard on radios smuggled into camp, that the war was over.

It took more than six months for the Tule Lake Segregation Center to close its gates, on March 20, 1946. Modoc County farmers immediately began to reclaim the land. Drawings were held in 1946, 1948, and 1949 to allocate a total of two hundred sixteen Bureau of Reclamation farm units to World War II veteran homesteaders. Some of these farm units were on land previously occupied and/or farmed by the evacuees. Each homesteader received one complete barrack from the former Tule Lake Segregation Center. Before the Japanese farmers arrived, the land had never yielded more than barley, alfalfa, clover, flax and potatoes. Some homesteaders tried to emulate the Japanese farmers' success growing sugar beets, strawberries, melons, carrots and celery. But they were never able to coax the same bounty from the land.

Some internees, with no resources left on the outside, stayed on until the camp closed in 1946. As the camp emptied out, Molly recalls her family being among the last to leave. It seems likely that Nobujiro took his time to plan for the family's future before returning to uncertain circumstances. Reports reached camp of Nisei veterans and their families being attacked, their homes burned. The Marysville District Chamber of Commerce had joined more than a dozen jurisdictions and many groups such as the Native Sons and Daughters of the Golden West in adopting a resolution on June 2, 1943, opposing formation of the 442nd Regimental Combat Team and any attempt to resettle Japanese on the

West Coast. Not until 2014 did the Sacramento City Council rescind its resolution adopted on May 28, 1943 opposing "the return of any Japanese (noted elsewhere in the resolution as 'Pagan' and 'undesirable') from concentration camps to their former locations." The WRA issued this unsettling advice for those leaving camp: "Whether you are within the barbed-wire enclosure or on the outside, there will always be the possibility of being caught in unpleasant circumstances. But it must be remembered that up to now a decidedly higher proportion of incidents involving physical harm have occurred within the camps."

On December 1, 1945 the Nakamuras packed up the same box the War Relocation Authority had issued them more than three years earlier, and boarded a train back to Marysville. There they found that only the Japanese families who owned land, like Nobujiro and Buntaro, had returned. Most Japanese business owners in Marysville had been renters. Molly recalls twenty Japanese stores in Marysville before the war. After camp, none of those businesses re-opened. The decades of prejudice, on top of incarceration, created a sense of dislocation that lasted years for many internees. "The young generation left after the war because they didn't have any employment," she says. "My cousin Frank was co-owner of Kirk's Pharmacy in Marysville before the war. He sold his partnership when the war came. Other relatives and friends left for the Bay Area, Sacramento, Southern California, or for other states. In my case my father owned a garage and rented it out. It was a residence too. My father and my uncle owned the Buddhist Church lot also. Across the street my father had rental apartments. So my father had all this income. He was lucky he had a good agent during the wartime, all three years. Some people had agents who did not pay them, and furniture they had stored in warehouses was lost. My mother-in-law's things were lost. My sister had four brothers-in-law who were farming, and one had his furniture stored in Freeport. It was stolen. Some people went home and found a mess. In Vacaville it was bad. The people were afraid to go back there."

The Nakamuras' home had been rented out during the war, but was vacant when they returned. The rent money was a stake that allowed the family to start again. Their old home felt like a different place, and the people Molly had grown up with were gone, but at least the family had a home to return to. Those who did not own land, or who came home to find their houses occupied by people who couldn't, or wouldn't, move out had to stay in hostels or churches while they looked for jobs and housing. The Marysville Buddhist Church leased its school building and community hall to the U.S.O. before the Japanese departed for internment. Now it became a hostel for returnees. In Sacramento the auditorium of the Buddhist Church (located at Fourth and O Streets at that time) became a hostel.

Nobujiro, as always, saw opportunity in the new generation of Japanese American households now forming. He and Motoyo began the grinding work of putting their home and business back together. "When I saw the Japantown in Sacramento after the war, it had gotten so dirty," Molly recalls. Nobujiro found carpenters to repair fire damage sustained during the war to his building at 317 Capitol Avenue in Sacramento. Soon he was able to send money to relatives devastated by the war and the bombing of Hiroshima. "I had a cousin whose son was born developmentally disabled due to radiation in utero," Molly says of one such tragedy. "My father's fourth nephew was an entrepreneur. He invested in a nursing home. He contracted cancer. My father gave that nephew a thousand dollars after the war, and he built a home in a suburb of Hiroshima City. It's still there."

Motoyo and Joe lived in Marysville while Joe began classes at Yuba College on a scholarship, and Motoyo picked up where she had left off before the war, helping families who lacked basic necessities. The family was reunited in 1947 when Motoyo and Joe joined Nobujiro in a house at Riverside Boulevard and Seventh Avenue in Sacramento. "All the Japanese used to live in that area," Molly says. "They grew flowers and vegetables there. They are mostly all gone now. It was right across the street from where Channel 10 is now." Joe had graduated from the high school in Tule Lake, and went on to attend California State University Sacramento. The campus was then under construction, so classes were held at Sacramento City College. He graduated from CSUS and attended UC Berkeley, but his health problems continued. Katherine had married and moved to Chicago after Tule Lake. Joe moved there to attend the University of Illinois for a while. It didn't last, and he returned to Sacramento to live with Motoyo and Nobujiro.

1948: Joe Nakamura's Sacramento State University graduation photo. He graduated one year after Sacramento State's new campus opened.

Joe did odd jobs, took recreational classes and participated in community and family life as much as he could. When his tuberculosis was diagnosed, he went to Alum Rock Sanitarium near San Jose to rest and recover. TB was endemic all over the world until antibiotics were introduced after World War II. A strict regimen of bed rest, which could last a year or more, was the standard treatment. "They were still hiding TB at that time," Molly says. "It was a disease people didn't like. I used to drive my mother there every weekend to see him. I remember when I was breastfeeding my daughter, I still had to drive my mother there. My mother didn't want to tell anyone. That's how one family I know all died before the War. Mother, father, oldest brother and one older handicapped brother. They all died because they didn't want to go to the sanitarium. Only one sister survived. I had a girlfriend at Colfax who met her husband in the sanitarium there. She lived until her nineties. There was lots of TB before the War." One of Molly's cousins in Japan contracted TB, making him ineligible to serve in the Japanese military. "I remember my sister every month sent his tuition to attend military school in Kure. After he graduated he contracted TB, so he didn't have to go to war. He was about two years older than my sister. In the sanitarium he met his future wife, a lady whose father owned a box factory. He was adopted into that family." On her first visit to Japan, in 1965, Molly met this cousin for the first time.

Molly was twenty-one years old when the camp closed down. Her college plans had evaporated with internment, replaced by immersion in Buddhist faith and practice, and a thorough education in Japanese culture. Molly knew she wanted to continue with her studies, but she had to earn a living. The War Relocation Authority initially imposed travel restrictions, issuing permission for internees to return to their home areas only.

Those first months after internment were as uncomfortable as they were liberating, a feeling Molly describes as "peculiar". She had been confined for more than three years, watched day and night with never a moment's privacy. She had obeyed rules for when and where to eat, rest and be with her friends. "I was kind of scared to leave," she says. "We had been incarcerated in that desert country for a long time. I didn't know how the public would accept us. I think everyone felt that." It took effort for her to walk the streets as a free member of American society. The old anti-Asian sentiment was still much in evidence. She was not a prisoner but not yet quite free. Her feeling of dislocation at this time was constant.

Helen had moved to Columbus, Ohio with her husband and daughter. "My father wanted them back," Molly says, and the Iwasakis did move back to Marysville, where they rented a home half a block away from the Nakamuras. One of the Iwasaki brothers moved to the Palo Alto area to learn how to raise chrysanthemums; another moved to San Jose as a pharmacist. Helen and George soon joined him there, and Helen opened a beauty shop in their home. When George developed heart problems and suffered a mild stroke, Molly moved in to help Helen with the difficult task of balancing the needs of a sick husband, a young child and a business.

Molly was taking the first steps toward what was to become her new life. She renewed her interest in Japanese culture and began taking lessons in flower arrangement, tea ceremony, and sand painting. At the same time, she dusted off the business skills she had learned before the war. She had been one of the top shorthand students for four years in high school, and took bookkeeping and typing. She took a job as a typist at the state education agency. "Before the war, all Japanese state workers were fired. When they came back, jobs were restored. I worked for the state just to see what it was like," she says.

Her independence and self-confidence grew with each new endeavor. She worked as a typist at Camp Beale, where she saw many of the Hawaiians who served with the famous 442nd Regimental Combat Team. The all-Nisei unit was the pride of the Japanese American community. "They all came back to Beale, I remember," Molly says. "Some of the Japanese Americans assigned to the Philippines were subject to discrimination there. They were told never to walk alone. They were called *hapon hapon*, Japanese Japanese. That's what the soldiers told us." At Beale, Molly was in the center of post-war activity in northern California. Camp Beale was established in 1942 to support the war effort; it became a U.S. Air Force Base in 1951. A history of the post notes that: "During World War II and for two years afterward, more service men and women may have been at Beale than at any other Army post. It served as a personnel replacement depot, which meant that soldiers were sent to Beale temporarily while waiting for their assignments. By September 1945, Camp Beale's Personnel Replacement Depot had sent over 225,000 men overseas. …Camp Beale was also a Separation Center, which discharged 387,174 men and women before it closed in April 1947."

In February of 1947, Molly took her savings from her job at Camp Beale and sailed on the Matsonia to Hawaii, a four and a half day trip, to visit Raymond and Mineyo Yamagata. Raymond was one of the Hawaiian mechanics who had worked for her father before the war. Although he wanted to settle in Marysville, he had returned to the family home near Waikiki, where he became a firefighter. He was happy to show Molly the sights. Her brother Joe's battle with tuberculosis piqued her interest in Kula Hospital, a tuberculosis sanitarium on the pleasant, southwest slope of Haleakala, on Maui. In Honolulu, she attended a festival where a veteran named Daniel Inouye was greeting the crowd on his first political campaign. Inouye, a member of the 442nd Regimental Combat Team, had been seriously wounded in combat and lost his right arm. He overcame both discrimination and injury to become a powerful member of the U.S. Senate, where he served nine terms.

Molly clearly recalls the evidence of devastation caused by a tsunami that had struck Hawaii the year before her visit. The largest and most destructive tsunami waves in reported history at the time were generated by an earthquake with a recorded magnitude of 7.8 in the Aleutian Islands off Alaska early in the morning on April 1, 1946. (The 2011 Great East Japan Earthquake was a magnitude 9.0.)

The tsunami struck Hawaii almost five hours later, killing one hundred fifty-nine people. Many were curious onlookers, including school children who ventured into the exposed reef area, not knowing the receding water to be a sign of an approaching tsunami. Waves in some areas penetrated more than half a mile inland. On her visit a year later, Molly could see where the tsunami had taken out a hillside. "Half a block in the suburbs of Hilo was wiped out. I saw a refrigerator and washing machine still sitting in the middle of the street," she says.

On this trip, Molly played her biwa for appreciative Japanese-speaking audiences on all of the Hawaiian Islands. Bishop Fujitani of the Honolulu Buddhist Church had been incarcerated in the Amache internment camp with her Uncle Buntaro, who asked her to perform this service. The Buddhist Church sponsored her island travels and performances. "Right after the war, there wasn't a lot of Japanese entertainment in Hawaii. I appeared mostly in churches, and on radio, too. After the Japanese economy recovered, all sorts of Japanese entertainment became available. But at that time, there was very little in the Japanese language."

1950: Graduation day at Fashion Design School in San Jose. Mr. Yamamoto presents Molly her certificate.

When she returned to Northern California, Molly stayed for a while with Helen and George in San Jose. She took classes at a design school there, and on Helen's advice, went to Los Angeles to finish her training at the Model Fashion Design School. "I didn't like Los Angeles," Molly says, "but everything my sister said to do, I did it." She stayed on for three years to finish the course, learning intricate tailoring and the YKY Yamamoto proprietary system of drafting patterns. She lived with a girlfriend, Mishi Ichiba, renting a room from a Japanese family. The daughter of the family worked for *Rafu Shinpo*, the Japanese newspaper still published in Los Angeles today.

Returning to Sacramento, Molly worked two jobs at the same time, teaching fashion design while watching her father's store. Her father called on her bilingual skills often, and she began what became a lifetime calling, helping Japanese and English speakers communicate with each other. Nobujiro had a business at 1313 Fourth Street, where he rented the top floor to a dentist and a doctor. The dentist asked for Molly's help with Japanese/English translation. Her language skills were especially useful in a series of battles over ownership of her father's property. The City of Sacramento was booming after World War II. The state had already forced Nobujiro to sell his property at 307 Capitol Avenue for a redevelopment project. The city announced its own downtown redevelopment project in 1954. It included a plan to tear down and rebuild a fifteen-block area that included most of the city's Japantown. The plan was implemented in 1958, and the city forced business owners in the old area to relocate. Molly recalls that her father owned another building on Fourth Street before it, too, was claimed for redevelopment.

Several families bought property in the area from T to W Streets around Tenth Street. They encouraged former Japantown neighbors to start over in that area. Nobujiro's final property purchase was at Tenth and W Streets. Wherever he went, Molly says, "My father enjoyed business. After the war he would match make couples, sell them their rings, then after the wedding sell them their appliances and furniture." Books of wedding photos commemorate these marriages, pictures of strangers Molly has never met but whose mementos her father kept.

With the return of his business success, Nobujiro was able to accomplish something that had weighed on his mind. He brought the ashes of his little girl, Sumiyo, who had died of influenza more than forty years before, from Marysville to Sacramento to be with the family. "He found a burial spot in Odd Fellows Lawn Cemetery, on Riverside," Molly recalls. "He was kind of surprised that they would allow a Japanese to be buried there, but they were very nice. Later he helped other families reunite in this way too."

Molly's uncle Buntaro returned to Marysville with his family after the war. He remained a prominent church benefactor and Japanese community leader. "My uncle was a very quiet man, always smiling," Molly recalls. On December 24, 1955, the Nakamura family held its breath and waited as the Feather River, marking the boundary of Marysville's Japanese community, rose in a devastating flood. A levee on the west bank of the river collapsed about one mile south of Yuba City, sending a wall of water four thousand feet wide and twenty-one feet high cascading into Sutter County. One hundred thousand acres were flooded and thirty-eight people died in the worst disaster in the history of California since the 1906 San Francisco earthquake. Buntaro and his family survived, though they had to evacuate. The Buddhist Church was once again a temporary hostel, this time for nearly a hundred families whose homes and farmland flooded.

In her mid-twenties, Molly was in no hurry to join her peers who were busy finding marriage partners. She had resisted the lure of marriage while in Tule Lake. "I'm glad I didn't get married in camp. A lot of those marriages ended in divorce, because you didn't have any idea what people's character was. In camp you got sixteen dollars a month for a job, and couldn't go outside. So how would you know what someone was like? There were many Kibei boys in camp who had just finished high school in Japan. They didn't speak English very well. I had dates in camp. One guy was two years older. He was a sophomore at Fresno State. He came from Rower, Arkansas. His brother was from Japan, and some of the family wanted to go back." While some of Molly's suitors were persistent after Tule Lake closed, she was enjoying her independence. When she was twenty-eight, Molly met Kazuo Kimura at the Buddhist temple in Sacramento. A tongue-tied bachelor seven years older than she, Kazuo was completely different from Molly's gregarious father, and from the boyfriends who were pursuing her. "At our first meeting we just said hello. He didn't make much of an impression on me," she says.

1921: Molly's husband Kazuo at age four with his father, Tsuneichi Kimura

1939: Kaz as a student at UCSF's College of Pharmacy

Kazuo Kimura's parents emigrated from Wakayama Prefecture, where for many centuries the family owned a prosperous tangerine and persimmon farm. Without the economic hardships that forced so many families to seek their fortune elsewhere, most of the Kimura family remained in Wakayama, where to this day they raise and ship mandarins and persimmons to Canada. Kaz' parents, Tsuneichi and Tomie, were the only members of the Kimura family to move to the U.S. Before World War II, the family lived in the Union Hotel (now a historic landmark) in Old Sacramento. Two of his cousins became pharmacists at the large Taketa Pharmacy Company in Japan. Kaz continued that family tradition, and received a degree in pharmacy from the University of California San Francisco in 1940. Racial discrimination made it hard for him to find work, though he did manage to get a job at Ishii Drugstore in Japantown. Ironically, internment meant that he was constantly employed. He was interned at the Walerga Assembly Center just north of Sacramento before he was sent to Tule Lake. All internees with any kind of medical training were required to staff the camp hospitals and pharmacies. When the War Relocation Authority declared Tule Lake a segregated unit for dangerous elements, and families were allowed to transfer to other camps, Kazuo and his family went to Topaz Camp in Utah. From there, Kazuo went on to the Gila River Camp in Arizona, before he took the WRA up on its offer to allow Japanese internees to voluntarily relocate out of the restricted areas on the West Coast. He moved to Chicago, where anti-Asian sentiment was less prevalent, earned his license as a pharmacist, and found a job.

After the war, Kazuo returned to be with his family in Sacramento, and although jobs were still hard to find, he managed to get work at a pharmacy. Perhaps because he had already seen so much, he was a quiet man who stayed close to his parents. He was the only boy in the family, with four sisters. His mother began to worry when he reached thirty-five with no marriage prospects. She enlisted support from the minister's wife, who recommended him to Molly as "the type who wouldn't fool around with other women." Molly remembers, "His mother was very worried because he was already thirty-five, and she was pushing and pushing," asking the minister every day whether Kaz had proposed marriage, whether Molly would accept. A pharmacist friend praised Kaz to Molly at every opportunity. Helen and her husband, also a pharmacist, joined the chorus. She was invited to picnics put on by a Japanese pharmacists' group, mostly graduates of the University of California, San Francisco (UCSF) School of Pharmacy. "My marriage was more or less arranged by the minister," Molly says. "I said to my sister, ' Gosh, you're arranging everything! Husband too?' Finally I said what the heck, even though he was seven years older than me. I didn't care about getting married, but they were arranging so much. We never dated. Kaz was so quiet.

He was so shy. I had a lot of other boyfriends, but my sister had high ideals. She plowed into my head, 'You have to have a nice man with a good education.'"

With her sister and brother-in-law pushing, the minister acted as go-between and arranged the *yuino*, or engagement ceremony, held in March 1953. "A go-between was an old custom in Japan," Molly says. "My father bought a lacquer tray that even in those days cost a lot of money. On top of the tray were thick envelopes with fancy knots, each envelope representing one of the gifts presented on the occasion of the *yuino*." The Mokuroku, or list of the gifts, read:

Kinpou: betrothal gift money;

Naganoshi: smoothed dried clam. Longevity;

Tomo-shiraga: white linen thread. Living together until hair gets gray/white;

Suehiro: a pair of white fans. Hoping that the family will flourish;

Surume: a dried cuttlefish. Meaning forever;

Konbu: dried kelp. Meaning blessing with healthy children;

Katsuo-bushi: a pair of dried Bonito. Meaning a man's virility;

Yanagi-Daru: Traditionally a wine cask was given, but money to be used for sake has replaced it.

Nobujiro had saved the best for his exemplary daughter. The hand woven silk brocade cloth covering the tray was so intricate that weavers could make only an inch a day. The ceremony involved *baishaku-nin*, matchmakers, one for the bride

June 14, 1953: Wedding photo, Kazuo and Molly Kimura. Molly designed and sewed her gown.

and one for the bridegroom. Molly's father could not act as go-between for his own daughter, so Molly's matchmakers were Reverend and Mrs. Sensho Sasaki. George Takani, a distant relative of Molly's, and a fellow pharmacist, acted as matchmaker for Kaz. They met at a restaurant in Japantown. The formal ceremony included seating assignments for both sides. The matchmakers did all the talking. The Reverend picked up each object on the tray and recited its meaning for the couple.

Molly was twenty-nine and Kaz was thirty-six when they married on June 14, 1953. Molly wore an elaborate lace gown of her own design. A celebrity wedding held in Sacramento on the same day sticks in her mind: Pat Morita was married to Kay

Yamachi, a Yuba City girl. Morita was singing in San Francisco's Chinatown at the time, before he went on to Hollywood. Born in Isleton, Morita spent much of his childhood in hospitals with spinal tuberculosis. After internment he worked at his family's restaurant before landing a good job at Aerojet General. Unhappy there, he quit

June 2003: Molly and Kazuo: 50th Wedding Anniversary

and became a controversial stand-up comedian with the nickname, "The Hip Nip." In the 1980s Morita's movie career took off. He is best known as the kind-hearted karate instructor in *The Karate Kid*. The Sacramento Japanese community followed his long career with interest. Kaz and Molly's engagement party was held at Pat Morita's mother's restaurant, Ari Ake on Fourth Street, not too far from her father's store.

Kaz was an early member of the Senator Lions Club of Sacramento. Chartered in 1954, it was the first in the U.S. to be composed entirely of Americans of Japanese ancestry. In a speech on the floor of Congress in 2004, Congressman Robert Matsui, who was

1960: Kazuo Kimura, Senator Lions Club President, speaks on the occasion of the club's 30th anniversary.

1960: Congressman Robert Matsui speaks at the Senator Lions Club 30th anniversary event.

himself interned at Tule Lake as a young boy, noted: "I ask all my colleagues to join me in saluting one of Sacramento's most important and respected civic groups. ... Lionism is an active and effective medium for national and world service, exerting tremendous influence for national welfare, international amity and human progress socially, culturally and economically. For the past fifty years, the Sacramento Senator Lions Club has embodied all of the best qualities that Lionism represents. ... Today, the Sacramento Senator Lions Club is a vital service organization that is composed of civic-minded persons of both sexes and many diverse ethnic backgrounds."

Kaz was Chief Pharmacist at Payless Drug for more than thirty years. He was President of the Buddhist Church, and for the rest of his life was one of Molly's biggest supporters. She was able to pick up her *biwa* studies again after internment because Kaz drove her to San Francisco for lessons. "I could never have accomplished all that I have without him. He was an ideal husband and ideal father," Molly says. "He was also prominent in the community. He served as president of the Wakayama Prefecture Society. He received the top Buddhist title from the headquarters in Kyoto. When Kaz passed away in 2008 more than four hundred people came for his service." Kaz' ashes rest in the mausoleum at the Buddhist Church of Sacramento.

With his marriage Kaz took on lifetime responsibility for Molly's younger brother Joe. "My brother's life was never a full one. My father directed my sister and me always to take care of him using the proceeds from his properties. His will specified this, and when I married, my husband was appointed executor of my father's will." Joe lived to be seventy-five years old.

Kazuo and Molly bought property near Freeport Boulevard in 1955. It is a busy Sacramento neighborhood today, but at that time Japanese farmers still tilled open fields in the area. An irrigation ditch ran through their property. Four years later, Kaz and Molly supervised design and construction of a home, with plenty of room to grow the flowers, trees and shrubs Molly needed for Ikebana arrangements. Many Nisei settled in the new neighborhood. "All my furniture was from my father's store," she says. "The rug lasted a long time. I still have some of the furniture." Those furnishings, acquired from the last of her father's many businesses, are tied to her last memories of him.

In 1952, the California State Supreme Court ruled the Alien Land Law unconstitutional. Congress overrode President Truman's veto to enact the McCarran Bill allowing Issei to be come naturalized citizens. Molly's parents finally became U.S. citizens in 1953. They were in their seventies. "It was just a formality," Molly says. "They had to go to the class and learn to say the Pledge of Allegiance."

In 1976, thirty-four years after it had been signed, President Gerald Ford repealed Executive Order 9066, and proclaimed the World War II internment a "national mistake." In 1978, Nisei civil rights leaders were at the forefront of a campaign for redress. After ten years of commissions and studies, President Ronald Reagan signed the Civil Liberties Act of 1988. It offered complete exoneration to people of Japanese ancestry who had been wronged by incarceration, stating that the evacuation and incarceration were "carried out without adequate security reasons and without acts of espionage or sabotage documented …and were motivated largely by racial prejudice, wartime hysteria, and a failure of political leadership." The Act provided redress of twenty thousand dollars for each surviving detainee. "It's too bad that Congress didn't approve that earlier," Molly says. "Our parents should have received that too. My own parents were both gone by then. My father died of a stroke in 1969. He was eighty-five. Mother died in 1984. She was ninety-five. Some babies were born in camp just before the war ended and they received twenty thousand dollars too. I didn't think that was fair. Other people thought that too." Molly and Kaz were in their sixties when the checks came. Did it make a difference in their lives? Not much. Molly had moved on. "Kaz bought a car with our funds," she says. "Our station wagon was getting old." In the same year Motoyo died, the California legislature proclaimed February 19 an annual Day of Remembrance to encourage Californians to reflect upon their shared responsibility to uphold the Constitution and the rights of individuals at all times.

Although Molly believes her parents deserved better treatment from the government, she takes comfort in the Japanese community's warm feelings for them. "My father was always helping people. They appreciated him. At his funeral in Sacramento, four to five hundred people attended." She takes pride in the stories she still hears about her father's business sense. "A friend told me that when Japanese cars were being introduced in the U.S. my father wanted to have all the Japanese invest in Toyota. But by then it was hard to get people to invest together. He was quite a businessman in spite of the language barrier." After internment, Nobujiro was once again wearing those sharp suits. "Just before he died he had a new custom made suit," Molly says. "The new minister at the Buddhist church received it after he died."

The Kimuras had two children, born four years apart at Sutter Hospital. Both attended McClatchy High School. Sylvia, born March 29, 1954 lives in the Bay Area and works in a hospital as a biomedical engineer. Clifford, born January 9, 1958, attended San Francisco State College, and now lives close to Molly,

1968: Dedication of San Francisco's Japantown, and first Cherry Blossom Festival to commemorate the opening of the Japan Cultural and Trade Center. Tradition called for families with four living generations to be present and participate in the dedication. *Four generations, left to right:* Robert Nakaji, daughter Mayumi, and Marjorie Nakaji (Helen's daughter); George and Helen Iwasaki; parents Nobujiro and Motoyo Nakamura. Governor Ronald Reagan, San Francisco Mayor Joseph Alioto, and district supervisors were also in attendance.

where his business schedule allows him time to help her. Neither has married or had children, though both have a close relationship with their mother, and have joined her on visits to Japan. As a girl growing up, Sylvia was often featured in Sacramento newspapers participating in Japanese cultural activities.

It has been written that most Nisei didn't talk about their internment experience. Family members, historians and advocates have put forward many reasons for this silence. Molly says: "There wasn't anything to talk about. Most of the Nisei didn't want to share with their Sansei (third generation) children. That wasn't uncommon. I have shared with several high school classes. They didn't have much of a response. They asked me, 'How come you didn't speak up?' They don't understand that we were such a small minority. I may have talked about it more to the public than my own children. Maybe my children have learned about internment in different ways. My daughter reads a lot. They filmed a TV miniseries of *Farewell to Manzanar* in 1976 (based on the internment memoir published in 1973 by Jeanne Wakatsuki Houston and James D. Houston). The filmmakers were recruiting Japanese American students as extras. They paid for their expenses. My son took a bus to Tule Lake, where the movie was filmed."

CHAPTER FIVE

A Cultural Ambassador Is Born

By 1959, Molly had fulfilled most of her parents' and Helen's wishes. She and Kaz had built a house in the South Land Park area, where several other Japanese families would also settle. Her two children had been born. Her father's business was on firm ground. But she had a restless spirit and too much energy to settle into the life of a traditional housewife. The cross-fertilization of Japanese and American culture, suppressed by virulent anti-Asian sentiment before the war, was now underway. Molly's deep commitment to Japanese cultural art forms found an appreciative audience. Helen Mering, a young member of the Sacramento Junior League, approached Molly for help in raising funds for a proposed Fairytale Town. The success of Disneyland, opened in 1955 after several years of relentless publicity, sparked interest in communities across the country in building their own storybook parks. Fairyland in Oakland, opened in 1956, was an early model, though all of the parks were unique. The Sacramento Junior League joined forces with the City of Sacramento and a fifteen-member board of business and community leaders, including Molly, to open such a park in Sacramento. Helen Mering was director of public relations for upscale Breuner's Furniture, and the widow of a prominent Sacramento judge. She and Molly were to remain friends, and Molly went on to campaign for Helen's son Phil Mering's election to the Sacramento City Council. Fairytale Town's first brochure, printed in 1956, outlined its goals: depicting classics in children's literature, and being "among the child's first contacts with life and human relations.

Molly plunged into high-profile community work with zest and, many would say, courage. "I had just come out of relocation, with not much experience speaking English. I didn't know anything about American society. Gladys Latham and Marie Stebbins, who were teachers at Sacramento High School and Stanford Junior High, and Mrs. Walter Christensen were my coaches. They taught me how to act and what to say. I wrote it all down. I would go on TV to talk about the project. I would ask Helen [Mering] what she wanted me to say and she would coach me." In addition to publicity and funding appeals, Molly kept the records of funds solicited from the Japanese community, whose response was generous. The volunteer board raised $82,000 of the $107,000 cost of the project.

1961: Installation of the Japanese Garden at Fairytale Town. Sacramento Senator Lions Club maintains the garden.

1961: Girl's Day Festival, Fairytale Town. The Kimura family presented a Japanese garden stone lantern from their family collection.

Fairytale Town opened its gate in 1959 and is one of the few original storybook parks still open. Molly's work to make the Japanese community part of this lasting Sacramento landmark is memorialized in the only way that matters to the children who still enjoy the park: she got to name a fairytale. She sought the advice of Reverend Kosho Yukawa, minister of the Sacramento Buddhist Church, and together, they picked the fifteenth century "Tale of Urashima Tarō." It is the story of a fisherman who rescues a small turtle from torture inflicted by a group of children. Tarō sets the turtle free to go back to the sea, and then learns that the small turtle he saved is really the daughter of Ryujin, the Emperor of the Sea. Transported to the bottom of the sea, Tarō meets the Emperor and finds the small turtle is now the lovely Princess Otohime. Tarō stays with her for a few days, but soon wants to go back to his village and see his old mother. The princess gives

Fairytale Town Director Kathryn Fleming and Molly

him a mysterious box called *tamatebako*. It will protect him from harm, Otohime says, but he must never open it. When he goes home, his mother has vanished, and the people he knew are nowhere to be seen. Three hundred years have passed since the day he left for the bottom of the sea. Struck by grief, he absent-mindedly opens the box, and a cloud of white smoke bursts forth. He is suddenly aged, his beard long and white, and his back bent. From the sea comes the sad, sweet voice of the princess: "I told you not to open that box. In it was your old age."

The Japanese garden was completed in 1961, and today the Tale of Urashima Tarō stands alongside the all-American classics at Fairytale Town: The Cheese Stands Alone, The Toy Soldiers, the Old Woman in the Shoe and Jack's

Candlestick. Japanese people gathered donations to order concrete statues of the fishermen and turtle. Tak Tsujita, a Certified Public Accountant, was especially helpful. A Japanese nursery donated all the plants, and Senator Lions Club still maintains Fairytale Town's Japanese Garden. Molly's grandniece offered the ultimate recognition: "Auntie Molly, you must be very famous! Your name is up in Fairytale Town!" A 1979 history notes that between opening day of August 29, 1959 and March 1979, Fairytale Town welcomed 5,346,546 visitors through Humpty Dumpty's gates. Today, nearly two hundred thousand guests from more than ninety-one zip codes and twenty-five counties visit Fairytale Town every year.

March, 2009: Fairytale Town, Girl's Day celebration display sponsored by Senator Lions Club. Left to right: Kiyoshi Sanui; Jane Nakagawa; Molly; Ann Brady; Jenny Chiu Allan; Mary Ann Miyao; Jim Fuji; Gary Allan.

Molly was just getting started. At about the same time that she was raising funds for Fairytale Town, a group of influential women formed to promote Ikebana, the ancient Japanese art of flower arranging, in the U.S. Flower arranging became blended with devotion to an ideal in seventh century Japan. It developed from the Buddhist ritual of offering flowers to the spirits of the dead. By the tenth century, the Japanese were presenting their offerings in containers, and Ikebana became an art form handed down through generations. Early teachers were priests and members of the nobility. As time passed, Ikebana was practiced at all levels of Japanese society. Ikenobo Ikebana was founded in the sixteenth century and is the oldest school of this ancient art. Though she was still a young woman,

March, 2009: Fairytale Town, Girl's Day celebration. The doll collection in photo was presented to Molly's daughter Sylvia by her two grandmothers when she was born.

Molly's long and deep relationship with the Ikenobo School, begun as a twelve year-old and nurtured in Tule Lake, made her a natural choice to help raise its profile in the U.S.

U.S. chapters of Ikebana International began in Washington, D.C. Preparation for a Sacramento chapter was underway by 1959. Marie Summers was the wife of an Air Force major stationed at Mather Air Force Base. She had spent four years in Japan during her husband's deployment. Ellen Allen lived in Tokyo while her husband was deployed to Korea. As the wife of a major general, she befriended prominent Japanese women, including the father of the president of Mikimoto Pearls, the daughter of the founder of the Seiko Company, and the wife of the owner of a major Japanese magazine. Molly joined these experienced organizers, offering her help as a contact with Sacramento's Japanese community.

1962: Molly, far right, joins four other prominent Sacramento women reviewing an invitation from former mayor Bert Geisreiter to members of Ikebana International in Washington, D.C. He invited them to sponsor a convention in Sacramento.

1969: Molly, center, with Urasenke Tea Ceremony Master and his wife, on the right, during the 10th anniversary of Sacramento Chapter Ikebana International.

Ellen Allen suggested that the founding group in Sacramento name a panel of advisors. These included the manager of the Sacramento branch of Sumitomo Bank, Frank Kent; a representative of the Crocker Art Gallery, Burt Geisreiter, a former mayor of Sacramento and head of the Sacramento Convention and Visitors Bureau, and Mrs. Ruth Scott. Molly soon came to know the advisory panel members, some of the most influential people in Sacramento. "I was raising kids at the time, so I took their advice because I didn't know much about it," Molly says. "Marie helped me get into American society." Marie Summers and Molly Kimura are listed in the official history as the co-founders of the Sacramento Chapter of Ikebana International, the twenty-sixth U.S. chapter formed. The Sacramento Chapter's first meeting was held in 1962. While San Francisco houses the Ikenobo Ikebana International headquarters for the U.S., its own chapter was organized after Sacramento's was already underway. Molly and Marie Summers remained fast friends.

Ikenobo Ikebana teachers were scarce in Northern California, and Molly's teacher in Tule Lake had decided not to teach when she was released from the camp. With characteristic energy, Molly threw herself into the job of preparing herself to become one of Sacramento's first certified Ikenobo Ikebana teachers. In the 1960s, about three hundred teachers presented displays and taught at an

Ikebana Expo in New York City. Molly stayed on in New York for a month, and received her full teaching credential. "Mr. Yamamoto, the Headmaster's uncle and guardian, was impressed with my presentation," she says proudly. "I went through all three steps of learning during that time." With her teaching credential, she received the professional title, "Tofu."

"I was asked to be the U.S. director but I told them no. I couldn't leave my husband and kids and work in San Francisco." In 1962 the founders of the Sacramento Chapter sponsored the first regional convention of Ikebana International. Molly went to Washington D.C., to prepare. It was her first trip alone out of state, the farthest she had ever been from her tight knit community. It was an eye-opener. "It was the first time I'd seen so many African American workers," Molly says. "In California I knew only one African American student. Her father was Nathanial Colley, a big civil rights attorney. It was fun to see different people."

As the Sacramento regional convention got underway, Molly was as much diplomatic liaison as organizer. "In those days among Japanese Americans, women leaders weren't accepted. But I learned to do what was needed. I had to go the Japanese Consul General's office to get visas so the representatives could come to the U.S. for a few weeks." She found herself arranging itineraries and interpreting for high officials of the Ikenobo and Ohara Schools of Ikebana. The convention's workshops and displays filled the exhibit halls of the El Dorado Hotel (today the Red Lion Woodlake Conference Center).

Ikenobo Ikebana International became a lifelong commitment. Molly was Chapter President for several years. She has taught hundreds of students over more than fifty years, and has escorted groups of students to Ikenobo Ikebana Headquarters in Kyoto at least six times. "When I went back to Japan, taxi drivers would ask me, 'When did you to go to America?' They could see I was dressed differently. They thought I was a Japanese native who went to school in the U.S. We were taught in language school that Japanese language is spoken differently depending on whether you are talking to upper class or lower class. I tried to use my best standard Japanese when I went there. I knew how to be courteous. I have had people tell me I am not like a typical Japanese, who will not talk to you unless you have been introduced. I tell them, 'You have to speak up. Americans are very outgoing with strangers.'"

Molly was developing her own independent way of looking at the world, and with it, a pragmatic approach that allowed her to express her point of view even in difficult circumstances. That independence helped her make new friends and expand her business contacts. Throughout it all, the people who mattered most have supported her. She smiles broadly as she recalls, "My father was so proud of me. He wouldn't tell me that, but he showed it. He asked to be invited to a banquet for Ikebana International. My daughter is the same way. I hear from other people how proud she is of me, and she shows me in many ways."

1959: Molly, holding son Clifford with daughter Sylvia, standing, at the dedication of the new Sacramento Buddhist Church on Riverside Boulevard. When a new temple is dedicated, the children of the congregation form a parade to remind people of the Founder, Shinran Shonin, who was ordained at age nine.

That family support, and her successes in community work, shaped her response when Buddhist Church leaders came calling for help with a bazaar celebrating harvest season. The Sacramento Buddhist Church Bazaar began in 1947 as a social festival, where church members and the local Issei and Nisei communities shared food, memories and friendships. It was part of the community's effort to rebuild after the internment years. Before long, it grew to include exhibits and demonstrations such as Ikebana, classical dancing (Odori), tea ceremony, Taiko Drum Clubs and other Japanese cultural arts. In 1963, Molly was asked to take on the job of reaching out to involve the wider Sacramento community. "I said, 'I'm a woman. I don't want any criticism for the job I do. If you support me with the Japanese community, I'll do it.' They said I would be doing a benefit for the church, so they agreed. The festival was very small at that time, and they hoped to increase attendance enough to raise ten thousand dollars. I shared publicity responsibilities with Ray Takata, an architect. I was on radio and TV and newspapers doing publicity, and I would wake up at four in the morning to make sushi for the bazaar. I have been involved ever since." Molly was especially

1970s: Molly appeared on local radio and television stations to publicize the Sacramento Buddhist Bazaar.

proud when Mayor Walter Christensen designated the Japanese Buddhist Bazaar a citywide festival in 1966, affirming the Japanese community's part in the mainstream of Sacramento culture. The YWCA and National Council of Jewish Women cited Molly in 1963 for her cultural contributions, and in 1972 the *Sacramento Union* honored her as one of its Women of Distinction, commending

her for enlarging the Buddhist festival and opening it to the larger community and adding a cultural program to attract more people. In 2011, the Sacramento Buddhist Church Bazaar was one of the biggest festivals of its kind, with more than forty thousand people in attendance over two days. The church keeps statistics that indicate the volume of work involved. In 2011, more than ten thousands pounds of chicken teriyaki, a ton and a half of rice and five hundred pounds of noodles were served in two days. At age 90, Molly is trying to step back, taking on an advisory role. "I've been involved with the church for fifty years, thirty of those as Sunday school teacher, many as coordinator. I think a lot of old people don't have anything else to do, and so they cling to things they've always done. I don't mind doing something different to involve and develop the younger generation in the culture."

1975: Annual Japanese Food and Cultural Bazaar

Molly's language skills, contacts and outgoing nature made her a friend of one of Sacramento's most famous, and reclusive, citizens. Eleanor McClatchy, president of the McClatchy newspaper chain from 1936 to 1978, insisted on privacy. Since she was the head of the biggest paper in town, the *Sacramento Bee*, and hers was one of the richest families in the U.S. at that time, she generally got her wish. Photographs taken of her were destroyed, and a 1980 obituary in the *Lodi News Sentinel* noted: "Miss McClatchy shunned publicity. She never allowed her picture to be taken, and didn't state her age or even the names of the schools she attended. 'I am content to have people think I live in a cave and wear horns,' she once said in a rare interview." The youngest daughter of Charles Kenny (C.K.) McClatchy, she was studying to be a playwright at Columbia University when her father asked her to take over the family business. Under her leadership the company expanded its interests to six daily newspapers, four radio stations and one television station. She never abandoned her passion for the theater. During World War II she formed the Sacramento Civic Repertory Theater, a touring company to entertain servicemen at Sacramento's military bases. The company found a home of its own, with her help, at the Eaglet Theater in 1949. The Eaglet, located in Old Sacramento, became the main stage of what is today the Sacramento Theatre Company. It was through the theater that Molly struck up a friendship with this powerful businesswoman in 1962.

The Sacramento Civic Theater was putting on "Majority of One," the story of a Jewish widow falling in love with a Japanese man. Molly recalls, "The manager of Sumitomo Bank called me to help Eleanor. This was the year of the first regional Ikenobo Ikebana convention in Sacramento. I was so involved with the convention I didn't have much time to help. They needed music and props and help casting the part of the Japanese characters. A teenaged girl named Mabel Imai was taking dancing lessons at this time with the Hanayagi group. It was led by three sisters, the Takedas, whose family owned a fish market downtown. Hanayagi had the perfect costumes. I contacted Mabel's teacher to get the okay, and Eleanor contacted her for a part in the play. Yamato Gekidan group has been active playing Japanese folk music in Sacramento since before the war. I called the head of the group and asked him about the props. I knew him in Tule Lake, where he made beautiful sets for productions. He could be a stubborn man, but he was talented. He was married to my tea ceremony teacher in camp. His name was Pete Sazaki."

This production must have been especially important to Eleanor, who had ghosts of her own to overcome. Her uncle, Valentine Stuart (V.S) McClatchy, was a founder of the Japanese Exclusion League of California in 1920, and was a leading voice in the movement that ended Japanese immigration in 1924. When he died in 1938 his son H.J. took up the cause, resurrecting the virulent rhetoric his father had used in testimony before the Senate Committee on Immigration in the 1920s to argue for mass removal and incarceration of Japanese Americans in 1942. Eleanor must have wanted to avoid both the appearance and the reality of insensitivity in casting this post-war story of racial prejudice. The Sacramento production of "Majority of One" was a success, and Eleanor never forgot Molly's help. Soon afterward, Molly was hosting a dinner at a Japanese restaurant for dignitaries from Japan. "I mentioned the dinner to Eleanor McClatchy and said it would be nice if she could come and meet them. She did come, and all the eyes of the local dignitaries got big. They couldn't believe it. She never made an appearance like that. She even allowed a few photographs with the Japanese dignitaries. Mr. Norton was head of the color photography section at the *Bee*. He asked me, 'Molly, what did you do? We are not allowed to take pictures of Eleanor.' He told me that (First Lady) Pat Nixon and Eleanor McClatchy were coming out of an elevator when Mrs. Nixon visited Sacramento. The picture of Mrs. Nixon included Miss McClatchy, and he had to throw it away."

1985: Eleanor McClatchy (center, seated) at her residence. Left to right: Mr. Taniguchi from San Francisco, sponsor of Osaka Children's Puppet Show group; Molly; (fourth from left, standing) Frank McPeak, public relations director for McClatchy enterprises.

It seems likely that Eleanor McClatchy's friendship with Molly was just part of her rethinking of her family's anti-Japanese history. In the 1950's, Japan was reorganizing its public broadcasting system, modeled before the war on the BBC. General Douglas MacArthur banned international broadcasting by NHK, and redeployed its facilities and frequencies for what became American Forces Network. MacArthur's staff put out an appeal to U.S. broadcasting companies for up-to-date equipment to open the Japanese market for commercial television broadcasting. Eleanor went to Tokyo, and later told Molly that she was impressed by what she saw.

"If you did well, Eleanor would go all the way. I asked for help promoting two performances at McClatchy High School Auditorium. Miss McClatchy promoted three performances of prominent Japanese artists in Kabuki dance, and a children's puppet group from Osaka. The promoter used to be a Japanese bandleader. He belonged to a Japanese religion that promoted world peace after the war. It was called Perfect Liberty. He called me one day. He said he was trying to get this religious group's puppet theater to come, but American society in San Francisco was not recognizing this wonderful troupe. He couldn't get people interested. He said, 'I understand you have contacts with McClatchy. May I come and see you?' He showed me the brochures, and the puppet theater was in English, good for children. I approached Miss McClatchy and asked her about it. She said, 'Molly, you came to the rescue of our theater. Whatever venture you want to support, I will do.' She okayed it. The troupe came for at least six or seven years after that. Each performance was $2.50 and made a few hundred dollars. After expenses, Miss McClatchy donated the remaining funds to Ikebana International in my name. Sometimes at the performances I had to stand up in the front row because the show promoters wanted to recognize me. I wasn't applying for these opportunities that came up, one after another, but it was natural to me."

Her language skills and willingness to ask others to help her build cultural bridges drew Molly further into the role of cultural ambassador. She enjoyed making contacts everywhere she went. "I met Mrs. Morigiwa, wife of the manager of Sumitomo Bank, when we organized the Sacramento chapter of Ikebana International in 1959. One day I went to a program at the Governor's Mansion. I took along Mrs. Morigiwa, and she met Jerry Brown's mother Bernice there."

Contacts made in Tule Lake helped her time and again. Molly called on Pete Sazaki once more for his expertise with stage props when she coordinated a kimono show at the El Dorado Hotel co-sponsored by Senator Lions Club and Ikebana International. Molly wrote and narrated the script for the show, often staying up most of the night to make sure the words were just right. And as always, she learned. "Kimonos, you'd think silk is silk. But all these areas of Japan had different plants for natural dyes. I couldn't believe how expensive they were. This is because they had to plant special reeds for the dye. You can tell where a kimono comes from the by the color of the dyes. I'm always curious about historical roots. People from Japan appreciate that. They have said, 'You're the only Nisei I can talk to.' I tell them you have to understand our backgrounds. Before the war we were not accepted into American society."

In 1959 the North American Food Distributing Company asked for Molly's help as a translator for a famous Japanese cooking instructor. The Kikkoman Soy Sauce Company, the largest soy sauce producer in Japan, was expanding into the U.S. market. In 1957 the company established its first subsidiary outside mainland Japan, located in San Francisco, and launched a marketing operation designed to popularize soy sauce in the U.S. The company brought a glamorous chef, Madam Tomi Egami, to Sacramento as part of a publicity tour. Madam Egami was an instructor to the daughters of the Japanese emperor. She owned her

1997:
Groundbreaking
ceremony, Kikkoman
Corporation's
second U.S. soy
sauce production
plant in Folsom, CA.
Molly with
the Kikkoman
Corporation
President's wife,
from Tokyo.

own cooking schools in Tokyo and Kyushu and was the author of a book, *Typical Japanese Cooking*. Molly translated for her cooking demonstrations. "The head of the company knew me from church, where I was a Sunday school teacher," Molly says. Kikkoman's strategy worked, and the company now has a global reach in many product areas. One of its two manufacturing plants in the U.S. is located in the Sacramento region, in the City of Folsom.

In the 1970s, Molly founded her own business, the CKS Agency. The name came from the initials of her son Clifford and daughter Sylvia, with K for Kimura in the middle. She contracted with the Convention and Visitors Bureau providing guide service, travel arrangements and interpreter/translator services for Japanese tourists. "I would arrange everything, even make dinner reservations. The consul general's office also referred people. All the travel agents knew about me through

1970: Sacramento Convention & Visitors Bureau booth at the International Travel Agents Convention in Tokyo. Molly was the interpreter, and attended with Sam Burns, Executive Director, Sacramento Convention & Visitors Bureau. They met 150 travel agents. This was the first International Travel Industry Convention in the New Otani Hotel, Tokyo.

the convention center. I remember one dignitary came from Japan. We all had to dress sharp and pass inspection. He represented the Japanese treasury. I also did work for a winery in Santa Rosa, and for a nursery. Another job was for Campbell's Soup. They have a factory in Japan for the Japanese market. All these people on the tour were winners of a contest among store managers. There were about thirty of them. It was May, when rice fields are planted in Sacramento. The travel agent asked me to stop the bus. An airplane was planting seeds in the rice field. These people couldn't believe it. The fields were so much bigger than

The 4th Japan Congress of International Travel
28, Nov. ~1. Dec. '83

1983: The Fourth Japan Congress of International Travel Conference, held at the New Otani Hotel in Tokyo.

Japanese rice fields, where no one would even think of using airplanes. They were taking pictures. A lot of Japanese people used to work at Campbell's Soup after the war. I also worked for a San Francisco linoleum company that hired a lot of Japanese right away after the war, in August or September of 1945.

October 1993: A memorable limousine ride to the Mayor's Conference in Sacramento. Molly was hired as interpreter for the Osaka Chamber of Commerce President.

October 1993: Sacramento hosted the International Conference of Mayors and Chambers of Commerce. Left to right: Osaka Chamber of Commerce representative with Vice Mayor; Governor Suzuki of Tokyo; Molly, acting as interpreter.

"It was interesting to me to visit all these different industries. If I were just a housewife I could never have seen these places. It was cheaper for them to hire me than bring somebody from San Francisco. I could have charged them more but I wasn't out to make a lot of money." CKS Agency also helped many Japanese wives of U.S. servicemen stationed at Mather and McClellan Air Force Bases when they visited their families in Japan. Through CKS Molly helped Japanese American families adopt Japanese children placed in orphanages after the war. Molly worked hard to find the children homes as soon as possible, and she has kept track of how they have fared. "There is a Japanese saying: The three year-old spirit lives to be one hundred," she says. Her experiences have left her eager to help Japan and northern California discover each other. "Japanese media don't know where Sacramento is. They don't even know it's the capital of California. I think Sacramento should be on the map. Travel agents too used to ask me, 'Where is Sacramento?' None of them knew. I want people to realize what a big city Sacramento is."

2005: Hiroshima Prefecture Wheel Chair Dance Club, led by Sakae Nakai, came to California during their United States-Japan Goodwill Tour. Official visits were arranged with Governor Arnold Schwarzenegger and Mayor Heather Fargo.

Molly has served several terms as president of the Hiroshima Nikkeijin Kai (a prefecture benevolent society, once known as the Hiroshima Kenjin Kai). "The past president asked me because I spoke both Japanese and English to be the head of the society. I was reluctant because I would be the first woman to do it. Now we are not all Japanese, we are a Japanese American citizens club," Molly says. In the 1950s, children who survived the Hiroshima bombing were given green cards to come to the U.S. Three hundred of these children came to the Sacramento region; six hundred went to the Los Angeles region. They are a special group within the Hiroshima Prefecture Benevolent Society. Molly cites the story of one atomic bomb survivor: "One member for example was nine years old when the bomb was dropped. His mother was a volunteer at the Japan version of the USO, women giving their time to help lonely soldiers by giving food and talking with them. Masaaki Tademaru's mother was in Hiroshima doing that on the day the bomb was dropped. She was killed. Tademaru at age nine went all around the city on his bicycle to find her, but she had been cremated on the spot."

September 10, 2012: Sacramento Hiroshima Nikkeijin Kai Welcome Party for Hiroshima Economic Benevolent Society. Molly coordinated the visit of 33 Japanese business executives meeting with representatives of the Silicon Valley rice industry.

Molly with Masao Nagano, left, Vice President of the Hiroshima Economic Benevolent Society (and TV Hiroshima President); Kazuyuki Takaki, right, President of Hiroshima Economic Benevolent Society.

The benevolent society raised funds and did everything it could to help the immigrants who came after the bomb. Nisei society members helped them find jobs. Molly recalls that a Japanese confectionary at Tenth and W Streets hired two atomic bomb survivors as cashiers. "The new immigrants had to work all the time, and had no time to take advantage of the language schools here," Molly says. "I have had to conduct board meetings in two languages. We have two big events: a New Year's party, and a memorial service on the first Sunday of August for deceased veterans and members and atomic bomb victims. I translated for this service, so I was nominated to continue as president." In 2010, the Governor of Hiroshima presented Molly with a certificate of appreciation as the first woman president of the Sacramento Hiroshima Nikkeijin Kai, as well as for her efforts to promote Japanese culture, noting that under her leadership the club grew in donations and programs. The occasion for the award was the 100th anniversary of the of Southern California Hiroshima Kenjin Kai. Molly noted with pride that the Sacramento club was older, at 105.

1981: Matsuyama Sacramento Sister City Affiliation Celebration in Matsuyama, Shikoku Island. Left to right: Mrs. Ida Russell, Sacramento City School Board Chairman; Molly, acting as Interpreter and Matsuyama Sacramento Sister City Corporation Board Member; Miss Thea Stidum, Principal, Sacramento High School; Mr. Ryozo Murakami, Principal of Nitta High School; Mr. Takeharu Nitta, President, Nitta High School; Mayor Tokio Nakamura, Matsuyama City.

Growing up in Marysville, Molly heard stories about a doll exchange between American and Japanese elementary school children. A former American missionary to Japan, familiar with the importance of dolls in Japanese culture, organized the Committee on World Friendship Among Children. In 1927, its first project was to organize the sending of 12,739 friendship dolls, also known as

1985: Molly and Mr. Hanaoka, her second cousin on her mother's side. She met him by chance while attending the Jinan-Sacramento Sister City Conference in Albuquerque.

Molly with Ralph Sugimoto, President, Sacramento Matsuyama Sister City Corporation, at the Matsuyama Sacramento Sister City Annual Banquet, held at Mana Japanese Restaurant.

1991: 10th Anniversary, Jinan Sacramento Sister City Corporation in Jinan. Molly was a Charter Member. Among the Sacramento Delegation, 2nd Row from Top: Dan Gorfain, President; Margaret Wong; Molly; Sacramento Mayor Anne Rudin; Dolly Louie; Supervisor Illa Collin; Roger Fong.

American blue-eyed dolls, to Japan. The dolls arrived in time for *Hinamatsuri*, the annual Japanese doll festival. "In Japan they used to sing a song, 'Blue-eyed dolls, how beautiful they are,'" Molly says. This act of goodwill inspired a Japanese viscount to reciprocate. The best doll makers in Japan were commissioned to produce fifty-eight friendship dolls, each dressed in beautiful silk kimono with unique accessories, representing prefectures, cities or regions. The dolls were sent to libraries and museums throughout the United States. The exchange continued after the war, when the dolls became known as "Peace Dolls." In the 1980s, Dr. Kawabata, a Japanese professor and a member of a society of doll collectors, asked for Molly's help as a translator. "Through him I met a woman in Boston who paid my expenses to be her guide and interpreter. She wrote poetry in Japanese. I visited collections in Boston that had saved all these exchanged dolls I had heard about growing up."

Molly's list of accomplishments chronicles her broad range of interests and abilities over the decades, always with the theme of building a cultural bridge between Japan and the U.S. She is a charter member of the Matsuyama, Sacramento Sister City exchange, and of the Jinan, China Sacramento Sister City exchange. She coordinated UC Davis Extension courses on Japanese culture, attended by two hundred educators from cities throughout Northern California. She coordinated a 1996 planting of Japanese cherry trees at Belle Cooledge Park. She serves as trip coordinator, interpreter and narrator for many visiting Japanese artists, musicians and dancers.

May 5, 1996: Dedication of sakura trees donated by Dr. and Mrs. Yoshihiro Hamaguchi, at Belle Cooledge Park. Molly coordinated the ceremony. In attendance were City Council Member Jimmie Yee, Mrs. Atsuko Hamaguchi, Masaaki Hamaguchi, Mrs. Masako Hamaguchi, and Dr. and Mrs. Yishihiro Hamaguchi.

Molly has earned teaching certification in the arts of biwa and *suna-e* (sand painting). A dedicated teacher of Ikebana, she taught classes at American River College for thirty years. She also taught Ikebana at the Marysville Buddhist Church, at the County Recreation Center, the Asian Community Center and in her home. She has demonstrated Ikebana and other Japanese cultural arts at schools, colleges, garden clubs, museums and service clubs throughout Northern California. In 1998 she was invited to Quito, Equador to celebrate and conduct workshops for Ecuador Ikebana International's tenth anniversary.

Molly has performed *Chikuzen biwa* at concerts throughout California. In 1997, she met the Japanese Ambassador while performing at the Japanese Embassy Theater as part of the Washington D.C. Cherry Blossom Festival. In 2010, she was a featured performer at a program titled: "Hidden Legacy: Tribute to Teachers of Japanese Traditional Arts in the War Relocation Authority Camps," held at the Koyasan Buddhist Temple in Los Angeles. It was sponsored by the University of California's Berkeley and Los Angeles campuses. The program noted, "... the beautiful Japanese performing arts ... were a part of life in the concentration camps – and brought hope, culture, joy and entertainment to the families who were incarcerated during World War II. ...They succeeded in keeping alive this heritage for future generations." Molly is one of the last remaining *biwa* teachers in the U.S.

In 1966, on one of her many trips to Japan, this time for Ikebana International's Seventh Annual World Conference in Nagoya, a history teacher at Nagoya Aichi Prefecture high school had a special request. The teacher, Mr. Tadashi Tsutsui, asked Molly to conduct a *biwa* performance and talk about incarceration in Tule Lake. Using slides borrowed from the Nisei post of Sacramento VFW, Molly recounted camp experiences from days when she had been not much older than the students in her audience. The university-bound Japanese students were fascinated by what she had to say.

On World War II anniversary dates, television producers from NHK, one of Japan's national networks, have come to the U.S. to interview survivors of the atomic bomb, and later, on the sixty-fifth anniversary of the war, survivors of the internment camps. "When NHK first came here I translated for them because no other Benevolent Association chapter presidents spoke Japanese, and the producer heard about my bilingual background. When they came to interview camp survivors, people of Japan were just finding out about the camps. They wanted to know. I was interviewed by the Chief Director of the Cultural Department for TV Japan, known as NHK in Tokyo." The program is titled "Living Voices of Survivors of All Japanese Wars," including World War II. Her interview aired in 2011, and is part of a permanent video archive on NHK's web site.

Molly has greeted everyone from high dignitaries to young students, offering interpretive services and introducing them to Sacramento's opportunities and history. Her phone rings virtually every day with another request. She is still happy to say, "Every time someone comes to town, they say, 'Get hold of Molly!'"

On November 8, 2011, following an extensive qualification process including several hours of interviews, Molly received the Japanese Foreign Minister's Commendation for her many contributions in preserving Japanese culture. The award went to sixty-eight people around the world, including Ikenobo teachers in Switzerland and Moscow. Consul General and Mrs. Hiroshi Inomata in San Francisco hosted the U.S. conferment ceremony. Congratulatory messages from Japan included Governor Hidehiko Yuzaki, Hiroshima Prefecture; Forty-fifth Generation Headmaster Sen'ei Ikenobo; Second Headmaster of *Chikuzen Biwa*, Kyokushu Tachibana; and Creator of Yoshikawa Sand Painting, Kashu Yoshikawa.

The Certificate of Commendation said:

"You have been making great contributions to friendship and mutual understanding between Japan and the United States of America through your untiring efforts of promoting and strengthening our two countries' bilateral relations. In acknowledgement of such distinguished contributions, I hereby express my deep appreciation and present you this official commendation. July 28, 2011, Matsumoto, Foreign Minister of Japan."

The award brought Molly's life to a full circle: "The Governor of Hiroshima said, 'All the citizens of Hiroshima recognize you.' I mentioned in my thank you remarks that if my parents and my sister Helen were here with me, they would rejoice with me. I think spiritually they are with me. I think as an immigrant my father was so proud of me, without sharing it. He even took a photo and sent it to relatives in Japan. I didn't know that. To him, I think my accomplishments were his accomplishments too." With typical humor and modesty, Molly adds: "My niece said in her speech that I am a very eccentric and unique auntie."

Molly's first performance in Japan, at Nagoya High School. She borrowed the biwa from Nagoya lute teacher, Mrs. Doi.

Students at Nagoya High School watch as Molly performs biwa.

A Cultural Ambassador's Photo Album

1983: Kaz and Molly traveled to China, visiting the Great Wall of China and other landmarks. The trip was sponsored by the Chinese Buddhist Association in Beijing. Photo on left: Tour leader and interpreter Molly Kimura with Rev. Hiroshi Abiko, minister of San Jose Buddhist Church.

Molly also traveled to China in 1981 and 1985, and coordinated group tours from Beijing to Canton.

An Immigrant's Daughter

1978: Dedication of a statue of Buddha, at the El Dorado Hills home of Molly's Ikebana student, Dr. Thompson. Dedication officiated by the late Bishop Takashi Tsuji.

January, 1980: Campaign dinner for Secretary of State March Fong Yu. Left to right: Molly; March Fong Yu; Ruby Fong.

96

1981: Presidents of Japanese Camellia Societies attended Sacramento's annual Camellia Festival. Dr. Jackson Faustermann and Molly coordinated the visit. Here, the group admires Capitol Park.

March, 1993: Dedication of Mary Tsukamoto Elementary School. Congressman Robert Matsui presented the school with a commemorative flag flown over the U.S. Capitol. Mrs. Tsukamoto taught in the Elk Grove Unified School District in Sacramento for more than 26 years, and was a prominent Sacramento Nissei.

1994: Molly organized and narrated a Yukata (cotton) Fashion Show at the California State Fair Cultural Arts Building.

Molly with visitors Chiyo Yamada and her son, journalist Toshihiro Yamada. Toshihiro is a correspondent for the Japanese language edition of Newsweek Magazine in Tokyo. He is attending Boston University on a Fulbright Scholarship.

April 18, 1997: Japanese Embassy, Washington, D.C. Molly; Ambassador Kunihiko Saito; Shizumi Manale (choreographer and dancer, Kodomo Dance Troupe).

Chikuzen Biwa

1970: Kyokuto Molly Kimura playing Chikuzen Biwa.

1971: Cherry blossom performance at Kabuki Hotel in San Francisco. Performing is Mrs. Kyokusui Yamasaki of Osaka, Japan. The Japanese government awarded her the "Biwa Living Treasure" title. Also pictured, Mrs. K. Itatani, of Hiroshima, Japan.

1971: Kyokuto Molly Kimura with Instructor, Kyokuso Yamamoto, in San Francisco.

1972: San Francisco Cherry Blossom Festival. Living National Treasure Kyokusui Yamasaki and K. Itatani of Hiroshima performed with students of Molly's biwa teacher, Kyokuso Yamamoto.

Students honoring San Francisco biwa teacher Kyokuso Yamamoto, seated, center. On top row, far right, is Setsuko Ishikawa, Molly's childhood friend and fellow biwa student.

Tachibana Kyokushu, Headmaster II of the Chikuzen Biwa.

Tachibana Kyokutea, Headmaster III designate, daughter of the current Headmaster.

1977: Molly was invited to perform biwa in Washington, D.C. for the Sakura Matsuri (Cherry Blossom Festival). This event commemorates the March 27, 1912 gift of Japanese cherry trees from Mayor Yukio Ozaki, of Tokyo City to the City of Washington, D.C. Molly also performed and lectured at the University of Maryland Department of Music.

Tea Ceremony

1962: Urasenke Tea Ceremony - Left to Right: Molly Kimura; Gyotei Nagai, Kyoto; Rev. Kosho Yukawa, San Francisco; Urasenke member. Mr. Nagai was the first visiting Urasenke Teacher in Sacramento from Kyoto, Japan.

1962: Molly with former Headmaster Hounsai's cousin, Kazuko Nishi, Tokyo, in center. She stayed at Molly's home for one month to introduce the Urasenke Tea Ceremony in Sacramento.

1965: Sacramento Chapter Urasenke members attending San Francisco
Urasenke Anniversary with Headmaster Hounsai.

1966: Urasenke Tea Ceremony demonstration at Mirian Stiehl's
home. Standing: Mirian Stiehl, Yoshi Takahashi, Alice Hayashi. 2nd Row:
Eleanor Vine, Molly Kimura, Toshiye Kakigi. kneeling: Linda Kakigi
Koyama, Mira Fong Nakano, visiting Japanese student, Sylvia Kimura.

1967: Former Headmaster's brother and the Urasenke Tantansai group receiving the key to the City of Sacramento.

1993: Molly shown in her interpreting role. The occasion was a visit by Hiroshima Governor Fujita to the Belle Cooledge Library's cherry blossom garden. Hiroshima Nikkeijin (Prefecture Society) sponsored a welcome banquet. Local Urasenke Tea Ceremony instructors and students served ceremonial tea to Governor.

Sand Painting

1967: Sacramento Mayor Walter Christensen designated the August Buddhist Church Annual Bazaar as a City Festival. Molly is standing next to Mrs. Christensen.

1967: Kashu Yoshikawa, Founder of the Yoshikawa School Sand Painting, holds the key to the City of Sacramento.

Molly with Headmaster Kashu Yoshikawa of Tokyo. Molly studied sand painting with Headmaster Yoshikawa, receiving her Primary Teaching Certificate and the professional title, "Shuto."

1970: Buddhist Church Annual Bazaar, demonstrating with daughter Sylvia, who also studied "Suna-E Sand Painting.

March 4, 1972: Sacramento Camellia Show. First Lady Pat Nixon accepts a sand painting titled "Camellia" by Headmaster Kashu Yoshikawa of Tokyo from Molly and her daughter Sylvia. Photo taken by Ray Iwamoto.

March 4, 1972: Sacramento Camellia Show. Molly presents a painting by Headmaster Kashu Yoshikawa of Tokyo to California First Lady Nancy Reagan.

An Immigrant's Daughter

110

CHAPTER SIX

Deepening Faith

Molly Kimura's spiritual journey began the moment she was born. "Hiroshima Prefecture is known as devout," she says. "My whole family was devout Buddhist, so religion was always being taught to us. Because of that environment, it has come naturally to me." Jōdo Shinshū, or Pure Land True Denomination, was established more than seven hundred fifty years ago and is one of the most widely followed forms of Buddhism in Japan today. As her mother was before her, Molly is a follower of American Jōdo Shinshū Shinjin Movement, started by Reverend Gyodo Haguri at his Fresno church early in the twentieth century.

"Through the primal vow of Amida Buddha, I went through the transformation of self-realization," Molly says. "I had my awakening at sixteen. Whether you come to awakening is dependent on your karma. Your mind undergoes a transformation, *shinjin*, which translates literally as 'true mind.' In simplest terms, you are awakening to the compassion of Buddha. There is a Buddhist concept of Virtuous Laypeople, who help you achieve awakening. My mentors included Mrs. Fukumoto. She was a farmer's wife, and a follower of Reverend Haguri's guidance. Throughout the rest of my life, many ministers guided me in compassion and wisdom so that I could share the Jōdo Shinshū teaching. These include Reverend Taikan Jinno, from Okazaki Aichi Prefecture, and Reverend Chikara Asoo, formerly head minister of San Jose Buddhist Temple. Mrs. Toku Nakawatase was a lay leader from Los Angeles who was sponsored by a Sacramento religious family to guide us every year."

August 1962: Rev. Gyodo Haguri started the American Jodo Shinjin movement at his church in Fresno.

Virtuous Lay Leader, Mrs. Toku Nakawatase, visited Sacramento from Los Angeles every year, sponsored by the families of Mr. Minoru Hayashi and his father-in-law Mr. Asano. Molly's daughter Sylvia Kimura is pictured with Mrs. Nakawatase at the Sacramento Airport.

May 13, 1977, in Kyoto: Molly with Rev. Taikan Jinno, from Okazaki Aichi Prefecture. The visit was sponsored by the families of Mr. Minoru Hayashi and Mr. Asano.

1983: Rev. Gyoei Nasu and his brother, Rev. Nobuo Nasu of Shiga Prefecture, at Enkyuji Temple, Japan. Rev. Novuo Naso sponsored Molly's ordination.

In the early 1930s, Molly's sister Helen Nakamura Iwasaki organized the first Marysville Buddhist Church Sunday school and Young Buddhist Association. When Molly reached high school age, she taught in the Sunday school. She credits her Buddhist faith with helping her to weather the discrimination that marked her younger years. "When I was a teenager, there was a turning point in life when I really was exposed to religion very deeply. We were taught that you have to accept things as they come instead of worrying or getting depressed."

Throughout her life, Molly has turned obstacles into an opportunity to learn. "As a teenager I found my culture very interesting. Some of my classmates said, 'Molly, I went to Japanese Language School as long as you did. How come you have mastered it?' My teacher was so enthusiastic about teaching me that she was very patient. I was this little teenaged girl. We liked to play around too, but I was very inspired by my teacher's talk and stayed with my studies."

Molly and Kaz in Kyoto with Dr. Aiyoshi Kawabata, center,
Professor Emeritus, Kyoto Medical University and a native
Kagoshima Prefecture. The Kimuras met him when he was
guest speaker at National Buddhist Women's Convention
in Sacramento.

Rev. Chikara Asoo, speaking here at a Sacramento dinner in
his honor, his wife on right. Rev. Asoo had been interned at
Heart Mountain, Wyoming, and was a teacher of the Jōdo
Shinshū faith.

In 1978 the Buddhist Churches of America (BCA) headquarters in San Francisco established a lay speakers bureau. Molly and James Iwata, both members of the Sacramento Buddhist Church, received a certificate from the late Bishop Kenryu Tsuji of BCA that authorized them to be lay speakers and visit temples in California.

One of Molly's most cherished accomplishments is her graduation in 1994 from the Nishi Hongwanji Chuo Buddhist Institute Correspondence Division in Kyoto, Japan.

Nishi Honganji was established in 1602 by the Shogun Tokugawa Ieyasu, and today serves as the head temple of the Jōdo Shinshū organization. Molly's sister Helen filled out the application for her admission to the school, acting on her long-held belief that Molly's path lay in the ministry.

Molly was the only Japanese American out of 362 graduates in 1994. Chuo Buddhist Institute required that she travel to Japan for three days after each year of courses was completed in order to receive credit. Coursework was conducted entirely in Japanese.

Molly taught classes on the Buddhist faith at American River College for several years.

平成2年度　富山別院会場スクーリング　H3.4.13〜15

1994 in Kyoto: Molly attended Buddhist seminars every year for three years in Japan in order to receive credit to graduate from Chuo Buddhist University, Kyoto. All of the courses were conducted in Japanese.

Three years after completing her correspondence course, Molly began ordination training. Reverend Nobuo Nasu of Shiga Prefecture Enkyuji Temple sponsored her ordination. The program included ten days of rigid training in a group of fifty-four. Molly describes the challenge: "We were not permitted to

十一月得度　受式記念　平成7年11月12日

November 12, 1995: Graduation picture, Chuo Buddhist University in Kyoto, Japan. Molly is in the center, 4th row from the bottom.

leave the compound until we completed the training. We woke up at 5:30 a.m., and were asked to clean all the compounds, cleaning the bathrooms and sweeping the yard. We had to rake and sweep up all the fallen leaves in the temple grounds, and vacuum clean the stairways. After that we had to go outside to exercise for about twenty minutes. Following that routine, we had breakfast. By that time it was about eight in the morning."

Morning services, lectures, examinations, chanting sutras and learning to conduct rituals filled the rigorous schedule until about eleven at night. In November 1995, Molly was ordained as a Jōdo Shin minister. The *tokudo* (ordination) ceremony was held by candlelight at six p.m. in the Amida Hall, in the Kyoto Jōdo Shinshū headquarters, and was officiated by Abbot Koshin Ohtani. The ceremony was at the same time of day when St. Shinran, founder of Jōdo Shinshu, was ordained at age nine.

1995: Graduation reception. Seated at left, Rev. Sannomiya, President of Chuo Buddhist University. Molly is third from left.

Today, Molly meditates daily at the same altar where she and her mother often chanted sutras together. She has conducted services or has been a speaker at many temples. She officiates at monthly memorial service, *Shotsuki Hoyo*, in Japanese and English for members of Sacramento Buddhist Church. She holds Howa/Dharma talks privately in her home, and is especially interested in teaching young people.

"I feel that teenagers have problems when they are neglected. A good teacher can inspire students. I know of two leaders, (Congresswoman) Doris Matsui's father and James Iwata, who were dedicated to teaching youth. Those two met at the Poston internment camp. They were very knowledgeable. They became Sunday School teachers (now called Dharma School) after the war. I learned from their experience. You can't just read, read, read about Buddhism. I determined you have to listen. Our Buddhist leaders all came from some kind of hardship. That's what young people can relate to."

Molly's special empathy in reaching out to teenagers comes not only from her belief, but from her own experience in her family. "I think all Asians have so much sense of pride," she says. "You expect your child to be a role model or good

2000: Conducting Memorial Day services at Marysville Cemetery for members of Marysville Buddhist Church.

child. It was the environment. My parents' and my sister's expectations made me a very abiding child, always doing whatever they told me. I always felt that I was in the middle."

Molly's directness and energy have drawn students who have come to her for dharma teaching for many years. Her Buddhist faith teaches an acceptance of the situation as it is, and making the best of bad situations. She points to the words of Shakyamuni Buddha: "Life does not go as we wish. The eight conditions that embody this condition of suffering are birth, aging, sickness, death, separation from beloved ones, not getting what we want, interacting with disagreeable people or undesirable events, and physical and mental disease."

In any life, and particularly that of an interned Nisei, these are familiar themes.

Molly officiates at monthly "Shotsuki Services" in both Japanese and English, in memory of families who lost a loved one in that month.

The spirit of *gaman*, a Buddhist term meaning to endure the seemingly unbearable with patience and dignity, was easily misunderstood by those who questioned how the Japanese bore the dehumanizing conditions of evacuation and internment. The Nisei were often seen as accepting of second-class status, and looked on with incredulity or distaste by those who did not go through internment and the process of rebuilding life afterward. In recent years, that *gaman* spirit has been re-evaluated in the aftermath of the devastating March 2011 earthquake and tsunami that struck Northeastern Japan. Reporters have noted that it seems the *"Shikata ga nai"* (it can't be helped) and gaman perspective, and the Buddhist teaching that life is impermanence and interdependence, have helped the victims endure the hardships and focus on the recovery process. They have even been credited with

2010: Molly presented at the Doubletree Hotel in Sacramento for the National Buddhist Women's Conference. Her lesson was that through Buddha's path (Butsudo), comes the art of Ikebana, Tea Ceremony, Calligraphy, Judo and Kendo (fencing). Calligraphy by Suiko Keiko Nishimoto.

helping the Japanese people achieve their famous longevity by lowering blood pressure.

At ninety years of age, Molly is frank about the obstacles she has encountered over the years. Like her father before her, she has found ways to deal with institutional barriers. In her role as an ordained minister, though not as a Buddhist Church official, she counsels the younger generation on Buddhist precepts. She tells them, "We need a spiritual search in this life. You have to know the difference between morals and spirituality, and you never know until you die in what condition you will leave this life. I'm a human too with so many passions. When you come to the end of life you appreciate wisdom and compassion. Buddhism is a way of life and it has always given me great energy spiritually. I like to share the wonderful teachings of Jodo-Shinshu, Pure Land Sect. I want to leave a legacy of my spiritual journey."

May 7, 2011: Molly Kimura officiated at a funeral service for her brother-in-law Ben Kunibe, in his hometown of Tahoe Keys. He was an active member of Optimist International, and his wife Terri was a Soroptimist. Three of Kaz's sisters are pictured: Machiko Kimura, Terri Kimura Kunibe, and Emi Kimura. Molly's mother Motoyo Nakamura's altar is in the background.

CHAPTER SEVEN

Epilogue: Looking Back

Is there an American story? This immigrant's daughter seems to have lived it. Born at home on a farm, raised feeling at home in her parents' culture, incarcerated for her ethnicity, struggling to find her place in a country that rejected her. She did more than overcome all of that; she set her own terms for living as a Nisei in post World War II America.

Looking back, she sees her deep Buddhist faith at work. "I have had a wonderful life. After the war I was in so many groups and associations. I assimilated into American culture." Her assimilation was a conscious choice, each decision leading to greater involvement as a cultural ambassador. Although she has a long history of service, she believes firmly that there is more to be done.

"The sermon I use for memorial services is for the Four Gratitudes: 1) to one's parents; 2) to all sentient beings; 3) to the ruler; 4) to the Three Treasures, Buddha, Dharma and the Sangha (Brotherhood). They used to have a course on *Shushin*, morality, in Japan. We need that now, the discipline to respect our elders and our parents, to feel gratitude for our country. Many in the younger generation are very independent, and accept negativity."

Molly believes there is no time, especially now, for negativity. "Shakyamuni Buddha depicted that the end of the twentieth century and into the twenty-first would be a dark era of violence. Even the weather would be violent. *Mapo* means the end of Dharma law, lots of sadness and violence. This is the reason I have advocated Ikebana, teaching peace through harmony, or as Ikenobo now says, 'Friendship through Flowers.'

I have blossomed because of all the contacts and people I have met. I have learned from all their experiences. As I reflect on my life, I don't have any regrets.

I have told in my sermons that we need a spiritual search in this life. My awakening has given me energy. What I'm trying to do now is to transmit that wonderful culture and heritage to the younger generation, not only to people of Japanese ancestry but to anyone who's interested. That is the work of the rest of my life." ❀

An Immigrant's Daughter

122

PHOTO ALBUMS

Senator Lions Club

Tezukayama Lions Club—Osaka. Sister Club of Sacramento Senator Lions

1993: Molly coordinated and interpreted for a series of Sacramento delegations to Osaka. Here, she gives a welcome speech.

July, 2002: Sacramento and Tezukayama Lions Clubs pose together in Osaka at the 20th anniversary, in celebration of their Sister Club relationship.

2008: 35th anniversary of the Tezukayama Lions Club, with delegates from Sacramento in Osaka.

Larry DelaCruz, a Senator Lions Club member and CEO of Veterans Benefits Insurance Services, has been a longtime friend and advisor to Molly.

2004: Sacramento Senator Lions Club President Molly Kimura on "White Cane Safety Day"

2004: (left to right) Outgoing Senator Lions Club President Hiro Tsuji, Mayor Anne Rudin, and Molly on the occasion of her installation as President.

2004: (left to right) Jerry Nakayama, Past President, Sacramento Senator Lions Club; Kay Fukushima, International Lions Club President; and Molly, receiving a plaque.

At the 2004 Lions Club Convention in San Ramon, California. Molly with International Lions Club President Kay Fukushima, and in a procession presenting the banner of the Senator Lions Club.

2008: Sacramento Lions Club Membership Chair Will Deguchi presents the Melvin Jones Award, Lions' highest recognition, to Molly.

Ikenobo

1963: Bottom row, center: Mrs. Hoka Nishimi, Ikenobo Ikebana School Instructor, with her students. Molly is in the top row, center.

1963: Molly displays her large classical Rikka style flower arrangement at the Shepard Art and Garden Center in Sacramento. She began exhibiting her arrangements at age 15 at the Marysville Buddhist Church.

1968: (left to right): Mayor Walter Christensen; visiting professor Tomoaki Yamamoto; Molly; Mrs. Christensen at the Ikenobo Ikebana Japanese Floral Art Show at the Shepard Art and Garden Center. Professor Yamamoto designed and exhibited a large Ikebana arrangement, shown center.

Former Sacramento Mayor Anne Rudin visited the Ikenobo Ikebana show, and here admires the free style arrangement Molly designed for the show.

Molly and friends attend a New Year's luncheon with students of the Sacramento Ikenobo Ikebana Tachibana Club.

1989: Fall Ikenobo Ikebana Exhibition with instructors and their students, held at the Sacramento Buddhist Church Hall.

1989: Ikenobo Ikebana Society of Northern California Chapter Anniversary Show, held at San Francisco Hall of Flowers. Ikenobo Headmaster Sen'ei Ikenobo from Kyoto was the honored guest and did a demonstration for chapter members. Molly was the interpreter for the show.

October 3-7, 1996: Molly and Kaz attended the Ikebana International Seventh World Convention held at the Nagoya International Convention Hall, and Aichi Art and Cultural Center in Nagoya, Japan.

Left to right: Mrs. Rinko Hana, President of Ikebana International Headquarters; Her Imperial Highness Princess Mikasa, Honorary Advisor to Ikebana International, and Mr. Lin Kohana, President, Ikebana International.

2001: 10th anniversary, Quito Chapter, Ikebana International. Molly demonstrates for Reiko Suzuki, wife of D. Suzuki, the Japanese Ambassador to Ecuador, and Mrs. Gail Cohen, wife of Ecuador's Ambassador, Enrique Cohen.

Forty-fifth Generation Ikenobo Headmaster Sen'ei Ikenobo demonstrated at the Eighth World Convention of Ikebana International in Yokohama, Japan. In attendance were, left to right, Her Imperial Highness Princess Mikasa; H.I.H. Princess Takamada; Noriko Matsudaira; and Kay Kramer of Ikebana International.

Top Photo: Left to right: Molly's assistant, Haruko Tocci; Kenneth Jones, interpreter for Headmaster Sen'ei Ikenobo; Molly; Headmaster Sen'ei Ikenobo

Chapter 50th anniversary at the Hotel Kabuki in San Francisco. Left to right: Mrs. Suimon Hane; Molly; Mrs. Shizue Watson; Mrs. Chiyoko Matsumoto. Front: Headmaster, Sen'ei Ikenobo. Mrs. Hane and Mrs. Watson were honored for their 77th birthdays; Molly and Mrs. Matsumoto were honored for their 88th birthdays.

2012: Head Ikenobo Ikebana Professor, Nobu Kurashige is Managing Director of Ikenobo Ikebana Society of America, San Francisco.

2012: Ikenobo Ikebana Society of Northern California Chapter past president, Mitsuyo Suiko Tao.

1980: Molly's free style arrangement at the San Francisco Exhibition included white birch tree branches.

2012: Students of Molly's Ikenobo Ikebana class at New Year's luncheon, held at the Lanai Restaurant in Sacramento. Owner Wes Kato catered the event.

2012: Molly's youngest Ikenobo Ikebana student Conor Mabary, studying with his mother Gena at American River College.

Molly and her student Ronda Huggins at an Ikenobo Ikebana demonstration presented at the California State Fair.

Molly designed a free style arrangement for the Ikenobo Ikebana Society of Northern California's 30th Anniversary exhibition at the Hotel Kabuki in San Francisco.

1994: San Francisco exhibition: Molly's free style design using unique materials

Ikebana International

1959: Sacramento Ikebana International Chapter Banquet. Guests (left to right): Japanese Consul Kubota (from San Francisco); Bishop, Shinsho Hanayama; Mrs. Kubota; Mrs. Hanayama; Molly; Bernice Reynolds, Pres. of I.I. Sacramento Chapter; San Francisco Japanese Consul and his wife; Judge Mamoru Sakuma

1959: Co-founders of Sacramento Chapter Ikebana International, Molly Kimura and Marie Summers

1962: Molly with Ikebana International President Ruth Scott, center. Mrs. Scott served as the third Ikebana International president from 1961 to 1963, and attended the first Ikebana International Conference in Washington, D.C. and the first Ikebana International conference in Sacramento.

1962: Ikenobo Ikebana Teacher Molly Kimura. Ikenobo continues a tradition of creativity that began more than 550 years ago. The Ikenobo headquarters is in Kyoto, Japan.

1962: The Ikebana Sacramento Chapter sponsored famous blind Japanese Koto musician Kimio Eto. A classical dance group from Japan and dance teacher Jutei Hanayagi performed a concert at McClatchy High School. Second row from the front, standing at far left is Frances Bogle, President, Sacramento I.I. Chapter. Front row: left is Jutei Hanayagi; second from left is Kimio Eto.

April 1963: Mrs. Ruth Scott, Tokyo Headquarters Ikebana International President presented a scroll to Governor Edmund ("Pat") Brown's wife Bernice at the California Governor's mansion. Pictured left to right are Headmaster Houn Ohara and his wife; Ohara School guest lecturer/interpreter Kodera; Ruth Scott; Mrs. Brown; Mrs. Brown's secretary; Molly on far right.

1963: Standing, left to right: Mrs. Soichi Nakatani, advisor; Molly; Mrs. Ashizawa, advisor; Mrs. Akio Hayashi, advisor. Seated: Mrs. Ellen Allen, Founder Ikebana International; Mrs. Bernice Reynolds, President, Sacramento Chapter, Ikebana International; California First Lady Bernice Brown. Mrs. Allen established Ikebana International headquarters in Tokyo.

May, 1963: First Regional Conference of Ikebana Internation in Sacramento. Molly and Kaz, pictured at left in the bottom photo, hosted a welcome dinner party at their home to honor Headmaster Houn Ohara and his wife. Molly's father Nobujiro Nakamura is pictured seated at far right in the top photo.

1963: Former Mayor and Director of Sacramento Convention and Visitors Bureau, Bert Geisreiter, promoting the first Ikebana International Conference held in Sacramento. Left to right: Past President, Ikebana International Sacramento Chapter, Susie Eisenhart; Mrs. Nakata, cooking teacher and Ikebana student; Bert Geisreiter; Mrs. Hoka Nishimi, Molly's Ikebana teacher.

Nov 3, 1963: Sacramento Chapter Ikebana International Festival of Arts

143

1964: Sacramento Chapter Ikebana International Meeting. Left to right: Sacramento Ikebana International Co-founder Molly Kimura; Bernice Reynolds, President, Sacramento Chapter Ikebana International; Mrs. Ellen Allen, founder of Ikebana International headquarters in Tokyo; Mrs. Shinsho Hanayama, wife of Bishop Hanayama, Buddhist Churches of America, San Francisco.

September 1969: Urasenke Tea Master Yamafuji Sozan, visiting from Kyoto, presenting a Tea Ceremony demonstration during the 10th Anniversary of the Sacramento Chapter Ikebana International, held at the Shepard Art & Garden Center. Left to right: Molly, acting as Master of Ceremonies and narrator; on stage are Chiyo Umeda and Peggy Mitutani, with Tea Master Sozan and his wife.

1970: Kimono Show at El Dorado Hotel, sponsored by Sacramento Senator Lions Club and Ikebana International.

1985: Eleanor McClatchy, seated, center, at her residence. Left to right: Mr. Taniguchi, San Francisco sponsor of Osaka Children's Puppet Show Group; Molly; Frank McPeak, Director of Public Relations for the McClatchy Company, and an unidentified man on the right. Eleanor McClatchy provided funding to the children's group through Ikebana International. They performed for several years in Sacramento.

Awards and Recognition

November, 2005: Molly, with Kaz, receiving the Sacramento Japanese American Citizens League (JACL) Community Award.

April 14, 2007: Molly with actor George Takei, who was himself interned at Tule Lake. The occasion was a gala dinner at the Japanese American National Museum in Los Angeles. Molly received the "Cultural Ambassador Award" for U.S.-Japan relations celebrating people-to-people connections, on behalf of Sacramento Hiroshima Nikkeijin Kai.

2011: Molly with late U.S. Senator Daniel Inouye and Mary Ann Miyao.

2011: U.S. Senator Daniel Inouye and his wife Irene Hirano Inouye, former President and founding CEO of the Japanese American National Museum in Los Angeles, with representatives of service clubs.

Foreign Minister's Commendation, November 8, 2011

Front row: Consul Takemichi Nagaoka; Setsuko Goldsmith; Tokiko Sunahara
2nd row: Sachiko Nodohara; Midori Ito; Hiroko Tsuda; Molly; Mayumi Ogui; Socho Koshin Ogui; Mary Ann Miyao
Last row: Virginia Uchida ; Alice Kataoka; Lynn Kurahara

Consul General Hiroshi Inomata & Mrs. Inomata presented the Japanese
Foreign Minister's Commendation to Molly.

Consul Takemichi Nagaoka and Hiroko Tsuda, Past President, Buddhist Churches of America Federation Buddhist Women's Associations, coordinated and planned the celebratory event for many months.

During the ceremony Molly was awarded flower bouquets. Left to right: Virginia Uchida, Molly's student in the Sacramento Ikenobo Tachibana Kai Club; Koso Nodohara, treasurer of the Sacramento Hiroshima Nikkeijin-Kai; Molly; Mary Ann Miyao, president of the Sacramento Senator Lions Club; Lynn Kurahara, president of the Sacramento Buddhist Women's Association; and Ralph Sugimoto, president of the Matsuyama-Sacramento Sister City Corp.

Sacramento Buddhist Church

2014: At the Sacramento Buddhist Church Betsuin. Rev. Bob Oshita presented a Letter of Appreciation to Molly. The letter was signed by Rev. Bob Oshita, Rinban; Robbie Midzuno, President of the Betsuin Board of Trustrees; Fusako Takahashi, President of the Sacramento Buddhist Women's Association.

Hiroko Tsuda; Molly; Rev. Bob Oshita, Rinban

August 9, 2014: Molly with Rev. Bob Oshita and Congresswoman Doris Matsui at the 68th Annual Sacramento Buddhist Church Japanese Bazaar

Molly Miyako Kimura
TIMELINE AND ACCOMPLISHMENTS

Timeline of Studies

Graduate of Marysville High School

Graduate of Marysville Japanese Language School – 15 years' attendance

During World War II lived at Tule Lake Relocation Center for 3 years

Graduate of Model Fashions School, San Jose and Los Angeles

Studied Ikenobo School Ikebana for over 15 years and received Teachers Certificate from Kyoto Headquarters and Ikebana name "Tofu"

Studied Chikuzen Biwa (Japanese lute) for 25 years and received Teachers Certificate from Tokyo Headmaster with Biwa name "Kyokuto". Most recently attained the Biwa name "Hokuin" in recognition of her accomplishments.

Studied Suna-E Sand Painting at Yoshikawa School in Tokyo and received Elementary Teacher's Certificate with name "Shuto"

1992 – Graduated from Chu o Buddhist University Correspondence Department in Kyoto

1995 – Received Tokudo (Buddhist Priest Ordination) from Nishi Hongwanji Temple Kyoto

1998 – Received highest Ikenobo certificate (Sokatoku) from Headmaster Sensei Ikenobo of Kyoto

2010 – Received Shihan certificate in Chikuzen Biwa from Headmaster Tachibana Kyokushu of Tokyo

Church Affiliations

In Tule Lake Relocation Center assisted in organizing Sunday school. After World War II, assisted in organizing Sunday school in Marysville.

Member of Sacramento Buddhist Church, Board Member of Buddhist Woman's Club, Sunday school teacher over 35 years

Past Superintendent – Sacramento Buddhist Sunday School

Past Superintendent – Northern California Buddhist School Teachers League

1978 – Appointed Lay Speaker of Buddhist Church of America by late Bishop T. Tsuji

Annual Church Cultural Bazaar Public Relations and Cultural Committee Liaison, MC and narrator of all Japanese programs for over 45 years

2007 – Served as President of Sacramento Buddhist Woman's Association

Cultural Affiliations

Taught Ikebana classes at American River College for 30 years until department closed

Teacher at Marysville Buddhist Church, County Recreation Center, Asian Community Center and classes at home

Demonstrated Ikebana and other Japanese cultural arts at schools, colleges, garden clubs, museums and service clubs throughout Northern California.

May 1998 invited to visit Quito, Ecuador Ikebana International Chapter to demonstrate Ikebana during their 10th Anniversary and conducted workshops for members

1997 – performed in Washington, D.C. Cherry Blossom Festival at the Japanese Embassy Theater, and gave lecture at University of Maryland East Asian Studies Department

1970 – Coordinated University of California Davis Extension course, "Japanese Culture" attended by 200 educators from cities throughout Northern California

1976 – Served on the writing team to compile a textbook, "Sharing Japanese American Diversity" sponsored by Sacramento Unified School District

1988-1989 – Served as a panel member for California Arts Council Traditional Folk Arts Program Grant.

1996 – Coordinated with Sacramento City Council Office and City Parks and Recreation staff for planting of Japanese cherry trees at Belle Cooledge Park. Trees were donated by Dr. and Mrs. Y. Hamaguchi of Japan.

Performs Chikuzen Biwa (lute) at concerts

Serves as coordinator, interpreter and narrator for many visiting Japanese artists, musicians and dancers.

Club Affiliations

Co-founder and past President, Sacramento Chapter Ikebana International with headquarters in Tokyo

Charter and Board Member, Matsuyama-Sacramento Sister City program from 1981-present. 2009 – Recognized with Honorary Membership

Charter and past Board Member, Jinan, China-Sacramento Sister City program

Former member of U.S. China People Friendship Society of Sacramento

1983 and 1985 – Tour Leader, Buddhist China trip

1983 – Served as interpreter for Sacramento Convention Bureau Manager, attending International Travel World Convention in Tokyo

Member of Crocker Art Museum Association, Sacramento Friends of the Library, Sacramento Zoo Society, Fairytale Town

Advisory committee of Sacramento State University Japanese American Archival Collection

Participant, Florin Japanese American Citizens League Oral History Book project. More than 35 Japanese Americans who were interned in relocation centers during the war. The book is on file in the libraries of California State University Sacramento and University of California Davis.

2002-Present – President of Sacramento Hiroshima Nikkejin Kai (first woman president)

2004-2005 – President of Sacramento Senator Lions Club

Awards

1969 – Sacramento YWCA Cultural Award

1971 – One of 10 selected to receive the Woman of the Year Award presented by the Sacramento Union newspaper

1987 – Recipient of "Kyogoku" Award for Outstanding Buddhist Sunday School Teacher

1991 – Recipient of President's Award from Matsuyama Sacramento Sister City Corporation for serving 10 years promoting friendships between the two cities

1991 – In Matsuyama, received Outstanding Service Award and gift from Mayor Nakamura of Matsuyama, Japan

1996 - Received Recognition from the City of Sacramento, the Mayor and City Council members for Outstanding Citizenship in coordination of Cherry Tree Planting Project

1998 – Recipient of San Francisco Cherry Blossom Festival AT&T Senior Appreciation Award from California Governor Pete Wilson, U.S. Representative Robert Matsui, U.S. Representative Nancy Pelosi, California Assemblywoman Carol Migden, and Supervisor Michael Yaki of San Francisco

1999 – Recipient of Service Recognition Award from Sacramento Buddhist Church during its 100th Anniversary Celebration

2002 – Received Recognition for service and Charter Membership Jinan, China-Sacramento Sister Cities Society

2004 – During Sacramento Chapter Ikebana International 45th Anniversary recognition, received award as Co-Founder of the Chapter

2005 – Recognition Award from Lions' Club District 4-C5 District Governor John Lynch

2006 – Received Melvin Jones Fellowship Award for Highest Recognition of Lions' Club

2009 – Interviewed by U.C. Berkeley Graduate Students of Journalism. Interview posted on Washington Post Web site, leading to an interview included in "Facing Japan" web site

2010 – Participated in "Hidden Legacy" event featuring teachers from World War II internment. Japanese Classical Dancing and Music Teachers' concert in Los Angeles sponsored by UC Berkeley and UCLA

2010 – Interviewed by Chief Director of Cultural Department of TV Japan (NHK from Tokyo) for "Living Voices of Survivors" of all Japanese wars including World War II. Aired in 2011.

July 28, 2011 – Conferment of Certificate of Commendation, presented by Takeaki Matsumoto, Foreign Minister of Japan, in recognition of "great contributions to friendship and mutual understanding between Japan and the United States of America through your untiring efforts of promoting and strengthening our two countries' bilateral relations."

2012 – During Ikenobo Ikebana Society Northern California Chapter 50th Anniversary celebration, participated in ribbon-cutting for exhibition at Kabuki Hotel, San Francisco, in honor of her 88th birthday

2013 – Interviewed by Susan Asai, Associate Professor, Northeastern University, Boston, regarding study of Biwa, for a book on music-making activities of Japanese Americans in California

RESOURCES CONSULTED

Of the excellent accounts of life in the Tule Lake Segregation Center, and of the events leading up to incarceration, these have been especially helpful in providing context for Molly Kimura's story:

Noboru Shirai, *Tule Lake: An Issei Memoir*, first published in Tokyo, 1981. Edited English version 2001, translated by Ray Hosoda. Molly witnessed most of the internment camp events included in this account.

Michi Weglyn, *Years of Infamy: The Untold Story of America's Concentration Camps*, University of Washington Press, 1996. (First published in 1976)

Brian Niija ed., *Japanese American History: An A-to-Z Reference from 1868 to the Present.*

http://www.Densho.org: The Japanese American Legacy Project, a digital archive.

The National Park Service web site on Tule Lake is expanding, and offers updates on planning efforts for the camp site as well as resources for teachers. http://www.nps.gov/tule/index.htm

The Sutter County History Museum has collected a rich repository of the history of the Issei and Nisei experience in Sutter and Yuba Counties.

Chapter One

Research of the International Nikkei Research Project, coordinated by the Japanese American National Museum.

American River Conservancy, administrator of the Wakamatsu Tea and Silk Farm Colony lands and museum: http://www.arconservancy.org/

Gary Y. Okihiro, *Cane Fires: The Anti-Japanese Movement in Hawaii, 1865-1945*, Temple University Press, Philadelphia, 1991.

Brian Niija ed., *Japanese American History: An A-to-Z Reference from 1868 to the Present*, Japanese American National Museum, 1993.

Conditions on Hawaiian sugar plantations:
http://www.sea.edu/spice233/hawaii_atlas/sugar_cane_in_the_pacific

Resources on hops ranching in the Wheatland area in the early 1900s:
Emil Clemons Horst: http://www.sacramentohistory.org/films_hopfarm.html
Ralph Durst: http://www.localwiki.net/yuba-sutter/Ralph_Haines_Durst

Labor unrest on Wheatland hop ranches: http://www.
sierranevadavirtualmuseum.com/docs/galleries/history/culture/chinese.htm

Wheatland Hop Riot:
http://www.newsreview.com/sacramento/hops-of-wrath/content?oid=455416
localwiki.net/yuba-sutter/Wheatland_Hop_Riot
A historical marker at the site of the riots notes their importance:
http://www.brightbill.net/cgi-bin/lm/one-site?site=68

Early census data:
Monographs Prepared for a Documentary History of Migratory Farm Labor in California, 1938, "The Parade of the Races in California Agriculture," Raymond P. Barry (Editor), Federal Writers Project, Oakland, California 1938
http://www.content.dslib.org

Chinese herbal remedies in the early 1900s: http://www.
sierranevadavirtualmuseum.com/docs/galleries/history/culture/chinese.htm)

Picture brides:
Japanese American Citizens League, South Bay Chapter Website
http://immigration.procon.org/view.resource.php?resourceID=002690

Kaga Maru ship's manifest: Archives of the Japanese American Museum, Los Angeles

Chapter Two

Alien Land Laws of 1913 and 1920, Santa Cruz Public Libraries: http://www.
santacruzpl.org/history/articles/147/

History of diphtheria in the U.S.: http://www.medindia.net

Buddy Uno: http://encyclopedia.densho.org/Buddy

Discussion of Shrine Shinto and its history:
http://www.asahi-net.or.jp/~qm9t-kndu/shintoism.htm

A history of Mather AFB: http://www.militarymuseum.org/MatherAFB.html

Chapter Three

A Central Washington University paper provides detailed descriptions of the
human and physical conditions in Tule Lake through the relocation years to
the present: http://www.cwu.edu/geography/sites/cts.cwu.edu.geography/files/
chapter6tulelake.pdf

Barbara Takei and Judy Tachibana, *Tule Lake Revisited: A Brief History and
Guide to the Tule Lake Concentration Camp Site*, T&T Press, 2001. This book's
discussion of the physical layout of the camp, and its transition to a maximum
security segregation center were especially useful.

Barbara Takei, April 19, 2013, "Legalizing Detention: Segregated Japanese
Americans and the Justice Department's Renunciation Program - Part 6 of 9"
http://www.discovernikkei.org/en/journal/2013/4/19/legalizing-detention-6/

Barbara Takei, "A Question of Loyalty: Internment at Tule Lake," *Journal
of the Shaw Historical Library, Vol. 19*, pp. 75-105, Shaw Historical Library,
Oregon Institute of Technology, Klamath Falls, OR, 2005. This article includes
an exhaustive bibliography of government documents and personal recollections
illuminating the complexity of the issues and feelings surrounding renunciation.

The Tule Lake Committee was created in 1978 as an all-volunteer, non-
profit organization. It has been instrumental in preserving the site, providing

education, and organizing bi-annual pilgrimages to the Tule Lake site: http://www.tulelake.org/

"From a Silk Cocoon: A Japanese Renunciation Story" is an award-winning film about one family's struggle: http://www.fromasilkcocoon.com/index.html

Chapter Four

A detailed history of Camp Beale and its unique place in military history: http://www.militarymuseum.org/Beale.html

Description of the 1946 earthquake and tsunami that devastated Hilo: www.tsunami.org/

An interesting history of the 1950s phenomenon of elaborate, Disneyland-inspired children's playgrounds: www.fairytaletown.org/

Obituary, Eleanor McClatchy, *Lodi News Sentinel*, Oct. 18, 1980

Chapter Five

Marysville Appeal Democrat, January 3, 2012, "Mid-Valley native honored for sharing Japanese arts, culture," Nancy Pasternack

Molly Miyako Kimura's Time of Remembrance Photo Gallery: http://www.bestnetsacramento.org/tor/tor_photos/molly_kimura/index.html

Washington Post's Facing Japan Series: http://www.washingtonpost.com/wp-srv/world/interactives/facingjapan/index.html

Chapter Six

An overview of Buddhist teachings and practices: http://buddhistchurchesofamerica.org/about-us/essentials-of-jodo-shinshu